PUPPETS

for

SPECIAL DAYS

By

CAROLYN LONDON

MOODY PRESS

CHICAGO

Contents

Foreword

Christian education teaches boys and girls, as well as adults, that the only right way to live is according to the plan outlined in the Holy Scriptures by an all-wise Creator.

Puppetry is an ideal means of making this plan vivid, impressive, and unforgettable. Puppets can easily portray Bible stories, morals, and ethics, and they gain force because they are never quite real—yet they seem alive.

In Christian education, the script is the actual teaching device, and what is said should give a deeper and more precise understanding of Christian truth. With an ever increasing interest in the use of puppets, the demand from churches for scripts has increased far more rapidly than the supply of useable plays. Therefore, it is most encouraging to have an entire book devoted to polished scripts, with each play designed to teach a truth. The educational value lies in the presentation; truths will be remembered longer because of the visual approach employed.

In *You Can Be a Puppeteer!*, Mrs. London describes various types of puppets and how to make and use them. She includes several complete scripts. Now she has thoughtfully extended your possibilities for providing happiness and blessing with *Puppet Plays for Special Days*.

DON AVERY

Introduction

"Let's do something special for Rally Day," someone suggests.

"Let's do something really special for Christmas," another person says.

A puppet show is always special.

The plays in this book are guidelines to help you develop your own story for a special day program. For the shorter plays, you do not have to have the puppeteers memorize every word. Let the children or whoever is doing the puppetry become so familiar with the story that they can put the puppets' lines into their own words.

However, with the longer plays, such as the "Three Pigs" and "Elijah and the Prophets," it might be advisable to record the play before presenting it. If this is done, the puppeteers only have to move the puppets to fit in with the speech pattern. It takes alertness on the puppeteer's part, though, to correlate the movement with the sound.

Unless you have very talented children, you will find that they tend to speak in singsong voices when reading a script. This can be overcome.

Most children are good at dramatics and will be able to enter into the feel of the play once they have overcome their

7

initial fear of a tape recorder. Practice on speech with the child so that he or she gets the general idea of it, then take the script away and let the child tell, perhaps in his or her own words, what has just been practiced. Record the speech, press the "pause" button, and rehearse the next speech, and so on.

The best way to learn puppetry is by plunging in and doing it. Don't wait until you have better and more equipment; don't wait until you've learned more; don't wait until— "Until" may never come.

You may want to do everything professionally right away, but you will have to learn by doing. Start with the shorter and simpler plays to develop your skills. No matter how unpolished you may think your puppet play is, it will enthrall your audience.

These puppet plays are more than just entertainment; they are more than just a baby-sitting job while the adults have their "real" service; they are more than just a time-filler; they are more than a diversion from the ordinary lesson. Those who prepare the presentation must realize that these puppet plays are presented to lead the audience, both children and adults, into the path that the Lord would have them walk.

Your puppet ministry is a spiritual ministry, and you must be spiritually prepared for it. Pray about your puppet shows. Pray with the puppeteers who work with you. Let them understand that the puppet show they are working on is being presented so that others can come to know the Lord Jesus as their Lord and Saviour.

May the Lord bless you as you present *Puppet Plays for Special Days*.

1

Christmas Puppet Show

A Puppet Play for All Ages

CHARACTERS

ABNER: older child
SAMUEL: younger child
FATHER
SPEAKING ANGEL
OTHER ANGELS

PROPS

CAMPFIRE: Make the campfire out of real twigs. The ends of the twigs that are supposed to be in the fire should be painted bright red, yellow, and orange. In the middle of the fire have either a red or orange lighted Christmas tree bulb or a small penlight with colored cellophane over the bulb.

TORCH: If you use a penlight for the campfire, you will need two for the performance: one to leave in the campfire and one for the boys to take with them for a torch. The one they take with them should be a very small penlight and

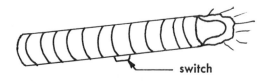

switch

Fig. 1a. Torch

should be wrapped in brown tape with red cellophane over the bulb. The switch can be left free, so that it can be turned on as the shepherd picks it up. (See Fig. 1a.)

SHEEP: The sheep can be made of absorbent cotton rolled and tied to represent sheep, or small toy sheep can be used. If the cotton is used, it should be fastened to the stage so that it is not accidentally moved by the puppets. The lamb in scene 2 (see Fig. 1b) should be made of something that is substantial enough to handle. It can be fastened to the side of the hill either by a projection on the side of the hill or by a pin. (See *You Can Be a Puppeteer,** p. 51.)

BRIGHT LIGHT: The bright light announcing the arrival of the angel is done with a flashbulb. Seconds before the bright light is to be seen, hold a camera with a flashbulb up to the stage. Then, as the father begins his speech, just before the angel's appearance, raise the flashbulb up above the level of the stage. (The audience will not notice this, as their attention will be on the puppets on the other side.)

At the appropriate time, press the flash button. An electronic flash is not bright enough and will not last long enough for the audience to really see it. Most cameras will flash without film in them; but, if you have one that needs a film in order to flash, either you can use an old

*Carolyn London, *You Can Be a Puppeteer* (Chicago: Moody, 1972).

out-of-date film, or perhaps your local camera store will provide you with a blank film cartridge.

ANGELS: If desired, the angels may also be lighted from within by having either yellow or white Christmas tree bulbs or penlights in them. These lights could be in their heads or under their robes. The angels should be *rod puppets* so that several angels can appear all at once on one rod. (See Fig. 1c.) The angels do not need elaborate features. Dots to represent eyes and red dots to represent mouths will be sufficient. They can be made out of white tissue paper or white gauze, with a little bit of gold tinsel attached. They do not need hands or wings.

Fig. 1b. Scene Two

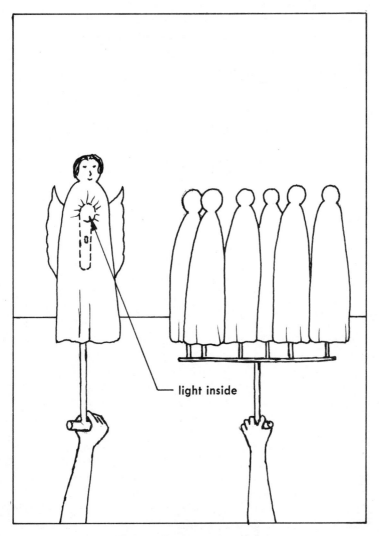

light inside

Fig. 1c. Rod puppet angels

12

(SCENE ONE: *Lights are dim, or a blue spotlight is used throughout. Father and Samuel move about the stage, touching the sheep and acting busy. There is a small campfire on stage, and several sheep lying down. There is a pot or jug near the fire.*)

FATHER: It is good to have one faithful son. I called your brother Abner, but he didn't answer. I even went into town looking for him.

SAMUEL: I don't know where he is, Father, but it is not like Abner to avoid work. Perhaps he just forgot. There are so many interesting people and things in Bethlehem these days.

FATHER: Your brother was just too interested in all the strangers in town!

SAMUEL: Some of the people have such rich caravans, but others arrive in town tired and hungry and on donkeys or even walking!

FATHER (*moving around and counting the sheep*): One of the lambs is missing! One of the lambs is lost.

SAMUEL: As soon as we have bedded the sheep down, I will go look for it.

FATHER: I don't like you wandering out on the hills alone in the dark. It is—

(Voice comes from offstage.)

ABNER: Greetings, Father. Greetings, Samuel!

(Samuel jumps up and runs to side of stage. Abner enters.)

ABNER: Oh, there you are! I saw the fire and hoped it was ours.

SAMUEL: Where have you been? Father is angry!

ABNER: I know. I'm truly sorry. I was so interested in the happenings in town.

(They walk towards the fire and Father.)

FATHER: So! You have decided to come.

ABNER: Father, don't be angry. I'm truly sorry.

FATHER: Didn't you know that it was time to come to the fields to shepherd the sheep? Didn't you know that you have a responsibility?

ABNER: Yes, Father, and I am sorry. I confess, I heard you call me. But I was so interested in the strangers who are arriving in Bethlehem!

FATHER: Well, you are here now, and that's the important thing. I will speak later of your punishment. There is one lamb missing. You and Samuel must go search for it.

ABNER: We will find it, Father.

FATHER: It is dark. Take a torch.

(Abner reaches into the edge of the fire and removes the torch. See Fig. 1b.)

SAMUEL: Come, Abner, I think the sheep must have been lost in the hills.

(They exit. Curtain closes.)

(SCENE TWO: *See Fig. 1b. The lights are dim with blue spotlights. There is a hill on the stage, and a lamb near the top of the hill. Lamb can be made out of cotton rolled into the general shape of a lamb, with a black nose and small black eyes. It can be fastened to the hill by a pin. See* You Can Be a Puppeteer, *p. 51. Abner and Samuel enter from opposite the hill, Abner carrying the torch.*)

ABNER: I am sorry that Father was angry, but I did deserve it.

SAMUEL: What were you doing in town?

ABNER: I was watching the travelers as I stood outside the inn. I heard one man tell the innkeeper that his name was Joseph. His wife was with him, and she was very tired. But there was no room for them in the inn.

SAMUEL: I don't understand why so many people had to come to Bethlehem.

ABNER: It's this new law the Romans have made. Everyone has to go back to the town of his ancestors and register. They will be putting new taxes on everyone, Father says.

But while I watched them, I began to think of the words that the rabbi read last Sabbath: "A wise son heareth the instruction of his father." So I left the town and came to the fields. I'm sorry that you had to do some of my work.

SAMUEL: That's all right, tomorrow I will let you do some of my work! Ah, it is dark here, and lonely. (*Pause, and a wolf howls.*) What—what is that?

(*The puppets cling together, frightened.*)

SAMUEL: Let's go back. Let's go back to the fire and Father.

ABNER: I have this torch. The wolf will not harm us. We must find the lost lamb. The wolf will like it for dinner if we do not find it soon. The lamb has strayed into very dangerous land.

SAMUEL: Do you remember that last Sabbath the rabbi also talked about a lamb that had strayed?

ABNER: Yes, I remember. He said, "All we like sheep have gone astray; we have turned every one to his own way; and the LORD hath laid on him the iniquity of us all."

SAMUEL: What does that mean?

ABNER: Father said the words were speaking of the Messiah who is coming someday, but I do not understand the words.

15

SAMUEL: It would be good to see the Messiah. He will deliver His ancient people, Israel.

(Wolf howls again.)

ABNER: We are going to need deliverance from that wolf! I think it is getting closer.

SAMUEL: And we are getting closer to the hill. It is so dark, it will be hard to climb it.

(They begin to "climb" hill. As they climb, one or the other slips frequently and is helped by the other. This is accompanied occasionally by words like "Careful" "Are you hurt?" by the puppets, and once in a while there is a wolf cry.)

SAMUEL: We are at the top of the hill, and I have not seen or heard anything of the little lamb.

ABNER: Sh! What is that?

(There is a very soft, faint "baaa.")

SAMUEL *(shouting)*: It's the lamb!

ABNER: Sh! I can't tell where it is. *(Looks over the edge of the cliff. Holds the torch over the edge. Sees the lamb.)* Samuel, I see it! It is caught in a thorn bush. Let me see if I can reach it. *(Leans over the edge of the hill and loses balance. The torch tumbles beneath the stage, and Abner "rolls" partway down the hill. He recovers and reaches for the lamb. It is a struggle, and he almost falls again and again. The lamb is bleating occasionally, and Samuel is calling, "Be careful.")*

Ah, there you are, you poor little lamb. Don't be frightened. Samuel and Abner have come to rescue you.

SAMUEL: It is so dark. Can you see?

ABNER: Not very well, but I have reached the little lamb. Hold me, and I will bring it up.

16

(Samuel grabs onto one arm of Abner, and Abner tries to get the lamb.)

ABNER: It will not do. I can't reach it that way. I'll crawl over farther.

(Abner leans over, and Samuel holds onto his robe. Then Abner takes both hands and releases the lamb. You must do it this way, for it is impossible for him to bring it up with one hand.)

SAMUEL: Careful! Do not slip!

ABNER: There, I've gotten it. Poor little lamb, you were lost and frightened, and you needed a shepherd to come find you. Now I will carry you back to the fire. I am glad that I did not stay in town, Samuel. Either of us alone could not have reached the lamb. It would take a strong, brave shepherd to do it alone.

SAMUEL: And one who was much bigger than we are, who could reach down from up high and reach the lamb.

ABNER: Now, let's hurry back to Father and the warm fire. The little lamb is cold.

SAMUEL: And so am I!

(Curtain closes.)

(SCENE THREE: *Same as Scene 1. Father is alone at the fire. The boys enter with the lamb in the arms of Abner.*)

FATHER: You have returned with the lamb?

(Boys draw nearer the fire.)

ABNER: Yes, Father, the lost lamb is safe.

FATHER (*moving toward them*): But, Abner, you are hurt.

ABNER: It is only a scratch. I received it when I reached for the lamb.

17

SAMUEL: It was dark, Father, and I was afraid. But Abner found the lamb.

ABNER: You helped. *(Places the lamb by the fire with other sheep.)*

FATHER: Sit down and rest. Here is some warm milk to drink.

(Hands Abner the pot. Abner drinks and hands it to Samuel.)

FATHER: While you were gone, my thoughts turned to one of the songs of King David: "The Lord is my shepherd; no want shall I know." Someday the Messiah will come, and He will lead His people gently, as a shepherd cares for his sheep.

ABNER: He will be the big, strong Shepherd who can reach His people and help them. It would be good to see the Messiah. Surely—*(He stops as a bright light appears. See special instructions.)*

ALL SHEPHERDS: What? What is that?

SAMUEL: I'm frightened! I'm frightened! Oh!

(Angel has appeared immediately following the bright light.)

ANGEL: Fear not. Fear not. For behold, I bring you good tidings of great joy which shall be to all people. For unto you is born this day in the city of David a Saviour which is Christ the Lord. And this shall be a sign unto you; ye shall find the babe wrapped in swaddling clothes and lying in a manger.

(Other angels appear.)

ANGELS *(singing or reciting)*: Glory to God in the highest. Glory to God in the highest. Glory to God in the highest, and on earth peace, goodwill toward men.

(The angels disappear.)

18

ABNER: Father, what was that? Was it really—

SAMUEL: Was it really—did we really see—

ABNER: An angel? Did we see the angels of Jehovah?

FATHER: It could have been nothing else. We have seen—

ABNER (*interrupting*): And heard the angels of Jehovah.

FATHER: We must hurry to Bethlehem and seek out this One who is born. We must seek Christ the Lord. Hurry, let us go.

(Begins to leave the stage.)

ABNER: But the sheep— Who will watch the sheep?

FATHER: The angels of Jehovah have told us to seek the Babe. Nothing will happen to the sheep. Perhaps even the angels will watch over them. Come, sons, tonight we have heard the messengers of Jehovah. Tonight we have seen His angels. Tonight the whole of creation is blessed. The Saviour, who is the Messiah, has come.

(Boys follow him off the stage.)

(Curtain closes.)

2

Thanksgiving Day

A Hand Puppet Play for Beginners and Primaries

CHARACTERS

ABIGAIL: a young Pilgrim girl
JOHN: her brother
LAUGHING WIND: an Indian girl

(SCENE ONE: *There is a fireplace with a big black pot and a painted fire on the back curtain. See Figure 2a. Abigail is working around the pot. She can pick up a piece of firewood and put it on the fire. This is done by turning puppet's back to audience and dropping wood beneath the stage. She picks up the broom and sweeps a bit, then stops and wipes her eyes, dropping the broom on the stage. Enter John. He lays some firewood on the stage.*)

JOHN: Sister, you are crying. Is something the matter?
ABIGAIL: I don't see what all the bother is about. Why should we have a thanksgiving celebration? This is hard work! Besides, what have we to be thankful for, anyway? Why should we have to work so hard just to have a feast?

Fig. 2a. Scene One

I would be more thankful if we could sail on a boat and go back to Holland. This is not our home. This is a hard country, this new world, and life is sad.

JOHN: Sister Abigail, do not speak such words.

ABIGAIL: Of a truth, John, I do not care. Life is too sad here in the new country. I am lonely.

JOHN: It is true we have suffered much loss and sorrow this winter.

ABIGAIL: With so many deaths—and even our baby sister lying in the grave— *(Cries.)*

JOHN: Sister Abigail, do not cry. Last winter was harsh, but this summer God has been good to us. The heavenly

21

Father has given us sunshine and rain, and our crops are good. Everyone will have food for the winter.

ABIGAIL: And now the elders want to invite the Indians to come and share our food.

JOHN: But they have helped us. And they, too, are bringing food.

ABIGAIL: What they will be bringing is more corn! Methinks I shall grow corn ears instead of my own ears! I am tired of corn. And I am lonely.

JOHN: I know that, since your very good friend Elizabeth died, you have been lonely. But here in the new world we can worship God as we please—

ABIGAIL: And sit on hard benches while Elder Smith preaches for hours and hours.

JOHN: Yes, but Elder William sees that you do not sleep! With that long wooden knocker of his, he knocks you wide awake.

ABIGAIL: Oh, Brother John, did you see that? I had hoped that you had not seen me fall asleep last Lord's Day. I was so very tired, and—

JOHN: And you began to nod, and Elder William just nodded his stick onto your nodding head. I must go. I have much wood to cut for the cooking fires tomorrow. Mother is baking much bread to take to the feast.

ABIGAIL: And Father has promised to shoot another turkey. At least we will have food to eat. I only wish I had a friend. I am so lonely!

(John exits. Curtain closes.)

(SCENE TWO: *Forest scene has several trees clustered together on two-thirds of the stage and some drawn on back-*

22

Fig. 2*b*. Scene Two

*drop. See Figure 2b. Curtain opens to find John with a
load of wood in his arms on the side of the stage where no
trees are. Enter Abigail.*)

ABIGAIL: I am getting hungry. I hope they hurry with the
food.

JOHN: I have just brought another armload of wood from
the forest. I am taking it to Father now. Soon the Indians will be here, and we want to be prepared.

ABIGAIL: I just saw Elder William and his wife. They were
bringing sweetmeats for the feast. Truly, he is more pleas-
ant when he has sweets in his hands than when he has a
wooden knocker to keep me awake.

JOHN: He just wants to keep you awake so that you can
hear the Word of God and be thankful.

ABIGAIL: I would be more thankful if I had a friend.

JOHN: Where are you going?

ABIGAIL: Mother wants more acorns. I am going to the

23

edge of the forest to look for some. We will decorate the tables with them, and tomorrow Mother will grind them into flour for acorn porridge.

JOHN: Don't go far into the forest. It is thick and deep and dangerous.

ABIGAIL: I know the path very well, thank you, Brother John. Just because you are my older brother and get to walk alone in the forest all the time does not mean that I shall lose my way.

JOHN: Just stay close to the edge, that is all I say. *(Exits.)*

(If you have a dimmer on the spotlights, they could be dimmed somewhat now. Abigail begins to walk into the forest slowly. She stoops every once in a while, as though looking for acorns.)

ABIGAIL: Brother John does not know anything. I wouldn't get lost. But I do wish I had a friend with me. I am so lonely here in this new country. I wish I had a friend. I really have nothing to be thankful for. Life is lonely and hard.

(Abigail is getting farther into the trees.)

ABIGAIL: It is so dark here. I—I am afraid. I'm lost! *(Cries.)*

(Lights are a bit dimmer.)

ABIGAIL: I am so afraid. I wish I had a friend with me. I hate this new country. *(Cries.)* I'm so lonely. Oh! *(Off-stage a wolf howls.)* Oh, what—what was that? *(Wolf howls.)* I'm so afraid. Please, heavenly Father, please help me to find my way home.

Home! Hm, yesterday I didn't think that our log cabin was so good. Today it would look very good to me. And how nice it would be to see my father and mother and Brother John. *(Cries.)*

(Enter Laughing Wind from the side of the stage where the trees are thickest.)

LAUGHING WIND: Do not cry, little white girl. What is the matter?

ABIGAIL *(frightened)*: Oh! Who are you?

LAUGHING WIND: I am called Laughing Wind. Do not cry.

ABIGAIL: How do you know my language?

LAUGHING WIND: My father is a friend of Elder Smith's, and he has learned some of your language. He has taught me. Tell me, why are you crying?

ABIGAIL: I am lost. I don't know the way home.

LAUGHING WIND: I know the way to your beautiful home made out of the wood of trees. I was coming to your settlement to join my father and your people in their feast of thanksgiving.

ABIGAIL: I am so glad you came. I was afraid. I prayed and asked the heavenly Father to help me, and He sent you.

LAUGHING WIND: Some of your words I do not understand.

ABIGAIL: Then you must come to see me every day, and I will teach you.

LAUGHING WIND: It is good. I will come, and I will be your friend, and I will tell you about the forest and the ways of my people.

ABIGAIL: And I will tell you about my people and about the heavenly Father.

LAUGHING WIND: It is good. Now walk this way. *(Laughing Wind leads the way out of the forest to the open stage and off stage.)*

(Curtain closes.)

25

(SCENE THREE: *Same as Scene One. Curtain opens to find Abigail and John both on stage.*)

ABIGAIL: I am very tired. It was a big feast and much fun. I do not think that I will ever want to eat anything again.

JOHN: It is true that there was much to eat. God has been very good to us and given us much to be thankful for.

ABIGAIL: Brother John, I am thankful.

JOHN: Are you thankful that you are not still out in the forest for the wolves to eat you?

ABIGAIL: I am thankful for that. But I am thankful for other things, too. When I was lost in the forest, I asked the heavenly Father to help me find my way home. This is my home, and I am happy to be here. I am happy we can pray to God and worship Him as He wants us to worship. And I am thankful for something else, too.

JOHN: What makes your heart thankful?

ABIGAIL: Today God gave me a friend, Laughing Wind. I found a new friend.

JOHN: Rather, the new friend found you!

ABIGAIL: Yes, she found me in a very strange place. Who would have thought I could find a friend in the forest?

JOHN: God has many ways of giving us friends. We never know when God is going to help us find a friend.

ABIGAIL: Or have a friend find us! I am thankful today because I have a home, because I can worship God, because God answers prayer and loves me, and because He has given me a friend to love.

(Curtain closes.)

3

Father's Day

A Hand Puppet Play for Fifth Grade Through Adult

CHARACTERS

STATION ANNOUNCER

MIKE READY: newsman

MR. LOVING FATHER: bearded older man

YOUNGER SON: young man

COSTUMES

HAND PUPPETS: They may be true to life or exaggerated. For example, the heads may be made of plastic balls or paper cups, or they may be molded doll heads. Dress the puppets accordingly, in biblical or contemporary style.

PROPS

STAGE: Puppet stage should be made to look like a giant television set. This could be accomplished by making it out of a huge cardboard packing box. (See Fig. 3a.)

Fig. 3*a*. Television puppet stage

28

(SCENE ONE: *Curtain opens to Station Announcer sitting at the desk with the microphone in front of him. Background could include a weather map.*)

STATION ANNOUNCER: And now, for today's weather. Whether or not you will like it depends on whatever you want to do. Today's weather for *(fill in your particular town or locality)* will be *(put in whatever is suitable for the day)*. And this is the weather for station TRUE's listening area.

(A message now comes up from backstage. This is a piece of paper stuck on wire. Station Announcer takes message off wire and glances at it.)

Ladies and gentlemen, in keeping with the usual alert practices of station TRUE, we now switch you live to the minicamera and our newsman, Mike Ready. Station TRUE has just received a newsflash that Mike Ready has been granted an interview with one of the wealthiest men in our area. Mike, are you ready?

(Curtain closes.)

(SCENE TWO: *Curtain opens to show white columns supposed to represent part of the rich man's house. Rich man has a beard. Mike Ready has a microphone, with wire [string] dangling from it and attached to his clothing.*)

MIKE: Good evening, ladies and gentlemen. This is Mike Ready. We are out here in the suburbs at the beautiful home of Mr. Loving Father. Mr. Father, this is a magnificent home you have here. As I drove up the driveway, I saw large herds of cattle and sheep. Most of our viewers would say that you are a very happy man to have such wealth.

FATHER: I am not happy. I would give all my wealth for just one thing.

MIKE: What causes this deep sorrow in your life, Mr. Loving Father? Perhaps the viewers of station TRUE could be able to help you.

FATHER: It's my son—

MIKE: But didn't I see your son when I came in? He was very busy. He was taking care of your herds. Surely he couldn't be any grief to you.

FATHER: It is not that son. That's my older son. He's always been a help to me. It is true, he isn't as happy and cheerful as he ought to be, and sometimes he's a bit surly. But he isn't the one I'm grieved about. I'm worried about my younger son. I don't know where he is!

MIKE: Surely—surely you aren't telling us that he's been kidnapped!

FATHER: No, he just left home. He left home—

MIKE: Did he run away?

FATHER: Not really. You see, several years ago he came to me and insisted that I give him the money that he would inherit when I died.

MIKE: That's a strange request.

FATHER: He—he wanted money more than anything else in the world. He thought, if he had his own, he would be free—and happy. But, I haven't heard from him in a long time, though I've looked for him daily.

MIKE: Ladies and gentlemen, this is indeed sad news that we are hearing from Mr. Loving Father. Perhaps, Mr. Father, if you could describe your son, the listeners to station TRUE might be able to help locate him.

FATHER: Son, son, wherever you are—if you can hear this

message, or if there is anyone who knows where you are—
please get in touch with me. Please! I've looked for you
every day. I've waited and watched. Please, please come
home—

*(Father's voice slows on last phrase. He raises his head and
motions with his hand for Mike Ready not to interrupt him.
At this moment on the opposite side of the stage Younger Son
enters slowly. Suddenly Father pushes Mike Ready to one
side and runs toward Younger Son.)*

MIKE *(excitedly)*: Ladies and gentlemen! Ladies and gentlemen, something is happening. Mr. Loving Father has
left this reporter and is running down the road. Yes,
something is happening! Stay with us, ladies and gentlemen. Station TRUE is on top of some breaking news.
Yes, a man, a young man is running up the driveway. Mr.
Loving Father and the young man are hugging each other.
The young man has fallen to the ground, and Mr. Loving
Father is lifting him up and kissing him.

MIKE: Just a moment, ladies and gentlemen. Can it be?
Yes, this reporter has just learned that the young man is
the long-missing son of Mr. Loving Father. One moment,
ladies and gentlemen, and we will try to get an exclusive
interview with both Mr. Loving Father and Younger Son.

*(Mike Ready moves to center stage where Younger Son and
Father are embracing.)*

MIKE: Younger Son, I am Mike Ready of Station TRUE.
Do you have a word for our listening audience?

SON *(voice broken and full of emotion)*: I—I just want to
say, I'm glad to be home. I left my father's house and
went into a far country. I wasted my life in riotous living.
I—I didn't know if my father would receive me or not. I

said, "I am not worthy to be his son. I will ask him to make me a hired servant."

FATHER: You're not a servant! You are my son! I love you. *(Walks a short distance and calls.)* Servants! Go kill the fat calf, and bring a new robe and a ring for my son. Bring him some good shoes. My son was dead, and now he's alive. He was lost, and now he's found.

MIKE: Do you have any message for the younger audience who are listening today, Younger Son?

SON: I—I just want to say, if there are any young people who have left their loving father, go home!

MIKE *(turning to audience)*: Ladies and gentlemen, this has been an exclusive interview with Mr. Loving Father and his prodigal son, Younger Son. We have just brought you one of the most dramatic news stories of the year. Stay tuned to Station TRUE for fast-breaking news. We now return you to the studios of Station TRUE in downtown *(your locality)*.

(Curtain closes.)

4

Mother's Day

A Short Play for Very Young Children

CHARACTERS

BASKET: a rod puppet, either a small woven basket or one cut from construction paper

TREE: a rod puppet, either formed of wire and crepe paper or cut from construction paper

NARRATOR: either a back-stage voice or the leader standing beside the puppet stage

(SCENE: *Curtain opens with a tree and a basket on stage. Scenery should be kept to a minimum: some grass perhaps, a river of blue cardboard along the back of the stage, but no other trees. See Figs. 4a and 4b.)*

TREE (*shakes itself and sounds sleepy*): I had a long nap. I was very tired. I slept a long time.

BASKET: It's about time you woke up. I've been wanting to talk to you.

TREE: Who are you? I never saw a talking basket before.

33

Fig. 4a. Front view of stage

BASKET: Well, I never saw a tree that could sleep so long, either. But, I'm very glad that you are awake. I was very lonely. It's lonesome now that the baby's gone.

TREE: What baby? I didn't see any baby.

BASKET: I'm talking about the little Hebrew baby. Pharaoh's daughter took him away, and I heard her call him baby Moses.

TREE: You'd better start at the beginning and tell me all about it.

BASKET: You know that the Egyptian soldiers have been trying to kill the Hebrew babies?

TREE: Yes, I heard about that. It's very sad.

34

BASKET: This baby's mother loved her little boy baby very much, and she made a plan to hide him so the soldiers could not find him.

TREE: What did she do?

BASKET: She made me. See how nice and safe I am? I can float on the water. *(Moves up and down the river.)* She made me very strong and soft inside. And she put the baby in me and told the baby's big sister to watch me.

TREE: Quick! Tell me! What happened?

Fig. 4*b*. Back view of stage

35

BASKET: Pharaoh's daughter came, and she saw the basket and found the baby. She liked him and decided to take care of him.

TREE: But won't the baby's mother be sad?

BASKET: No. You see, God had a plan for that mother. Pharaoh's daughter saw the baby's sister, and she sent her to find Moses' mother.

TREE: Tell me, what happened then?

BASKET: Baby Moses' mother took him home, and she will take care of him. Now the soldiers will not kill the baby.

TREE: Moses' mother must be very happy.

BASKET: She *is* very happy. She loves her baby very much. That's why she made me. She made a nice basket so that her baby would be safe.

TREE: I wonder if any of the boys and girls who are watching us have mothers who love them and take care of them?

BASKET: I wonder.

NARRATOR: Maybe you boys and girls would like to tell us some of the nice things that our mothers do for us.

(Curtain closes.)

5

Easter Worship Service

Musical Shadow Puppet Program

NOTES FOR SHADOW PUPPETS

Shadow play is not new or strange. Throughout generations, parents have made shadow pictures on walls for their children, and youngsters have entertained themselves with making shadow rabbits, alligators, and other pictures on their bedroom walls. The ancient Orientals perfected the art of shadow-picture making, using delicate leather puppets with articulated joints to tell the story of their gods and their relationship with mankind.

But shadow puppetry, although not unknown in theory, is often avoided by many puppeteers because of supposed difficulties. The equipment is simple: a room or auditorium that can be completely darkened, puppets with clear-cut silhouettes, a bright source of life, and a curtain. See Figure 5 *a*. The curtain can be a tightly stretched piece of bed sheet, or two or three layers of white tissue paper glued to a frame. Some window shades will let the light through so that good, clear shadows can be seen. Experiment to find out the size

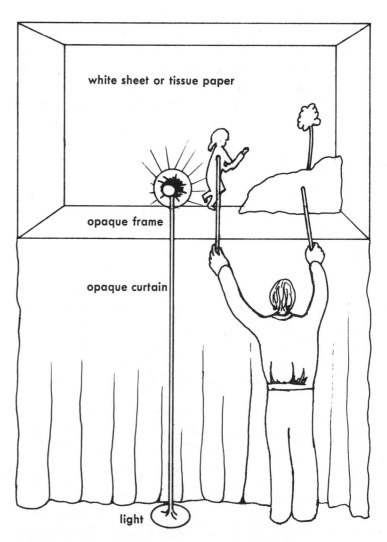

white sheet or tissue paper

opaque frame

opaque curtain

light

Fig. 5a. Back view of stage for shadow puppets

38

and type of screen best suited to your purposes. This will depend on the size of your room. Unless you are working in a very small room, your shadow puppets should be as least ten inches high so they can be recognized easily.

Rod puppets are generally used for this kind of presentation. Because the light diffuses the shadow of the rod when the rod has to be seen on screen, it is seldom noticed. Besides, the rod just "fades away" in the viewers' eyes, and only the puppet that is telling the interesting story is noticed.

In this Easter worship service, the rods, with the exception of those of the "colored wads," are never seen. The puppets are always at the bottom of the screen, and the rods do not have to appear. The silhouette or puppet should always be held very close to the screen unless you want the puppet to "disappear" or "dissolve." Experiment with the puppets so that you can work out the different effects for yourself.

No one can give you the exact directions for where the light is to be placed. This will depend on the size of your screen, the size of your auditorium, and the effect you wish to produce.

Most puppet stories have a great deal of movement. Indeed, this seems to be the main purpose of many puppet presentations. But your purpose as a puppeteer is not simply for action or for the entertainment of the audience. You have a *message* that you want to get across, and it is this message that is all-important. All of the plays in this book, with the addition of a few lines in some of them, could stand alone as stories or plays for human actors.

Some puppeteers believe that puppets *must* move, but if the quiet, still figure will best convey your message, then your puppet must remain motionless.

For this Easter worship service we have chosen only still figures, with the exception of the moving "colored wads." This will serve two purposes: first and most important, it will convey the solemnity of the Easter message; second, it will allow you to get the feel of shadow puppetry before working with articulated puppets.

Some Bible stories will adapt easily to shadow puppetry with motion. Jonah running away from God's purpose and entering a boat, the huge waves tossing up and down, Jonah being tossed overboard, swallowed, and eventually vomited up by the fish would provide not only plenty of motion but a visually exciting story. The collapse of the tower of Babel, Noah bringing the animals into the ark, the rise of the flood waters, the raising of Dorcas from the dead, and the healing of the cripple at the Beautiful Gate of the Temple by Peter and John would lend themselves beautifully to shadow puppetry.

SILHOUETTES

hill	hill and three crosses
star with yellow cellophane center	cross with red cellophane center
Jesus standing	tomb with removable door, yellow cellophane in door-
Pilate on throne	
colored cellophane wads	way

COLORED WADS: These are made of cellophane wadded into a loose ball about the size of a man's fist. They are wired to black rods (a straightened-out clothes hanger will do). See Figure 5b.

SILHOUETTES: These may be cut from heavy black cardboard. For interesting effects, cut openings in the silhou-

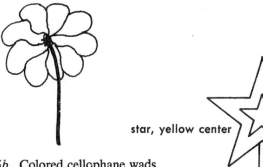

Fig. 5b. Colored cellophane wads

star, yellow center

cross, red center

tomb, yellow doorway

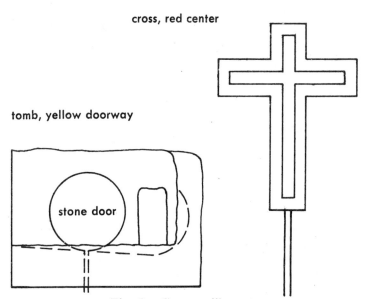

stone door

Fig. 5c. Cut-out silhouettes

41

ette and cover with colored cellophane. For examples, see Figure 5c showing cut-out star, cross, and tomb.

Worship Service

The Easter shadow puppet worship service is just what it is called—a worship service. The congregation should not be led to expect a fun-filled puppet show. The atmosphere in the auditorium should be of worshipful calm. Lights in the room where the puppet presentation is to be made should be kept as low as possible so that there will not be too much contrast when the service begins. Soft music should be played throughout the entire seating process. Easter Sunday night would be a good time to present this worship service to the entire congregation.

This program can involve both the adult and junior choirs and as many different readers as desired.

Program

Congregational Hymn: "And Can It Be That I Should Gain?" or your choice
Announcements and Offering
Congregational Hymn: "Grace Greater Than Our Sin" or "Wonderful Grace of Jesus"
Scripture Reading: Isaiah 53:1-12
Solo: "Turn Your Eyes upon Jesus"

SCENE ONE: *House lights dim. Curtains open to show the lighted shadow screen with the silhouettes of the hill and the bright star. (See Fig. 5d.)*

Choir: " 'Tis Midnight and on Olive's Brow" (first verse)
At the end of the first line, "The star is dimmed that lately

42

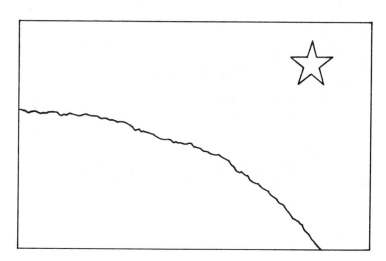

Fig. 5*d*. Scene One

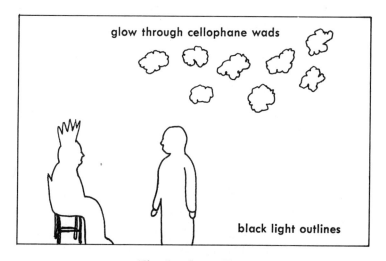

Fig. 5*e*. Scene Two

43

shone," the star, which has been close to the shadow screen, is pulled back so that it fades. It is then removed. While this is happening, in the upper right of the shadow screen, the silhouette of the Lord Jesus has appeared.

READER: John 17:1-26

CHOIR: " 'Tis Midnight and on Olive's Brow" (humming softly during scripture reading)

Lights behind the screen dim gradually, and at the end of the reading the shadow screen is dark, allowing a black silhouette of Pilate on a throne and Jesus standing to be set up for the next scene.

SCENE TWO: Screen is lighted to reveal the silhouettes. (See Fig. 5e.)

CHOIR: "What Will You Do with Jesus?" (first verse and chorus only)

During this song small children can be used to move the colored wads of cellophane behind the silhouettes of Pilate and Jesus. This will give the effect of colored lights playing in the background.

SCENE THREE: Lights out. Set up the silhouette of Jesus with the cross. (See Fig 5f.) Lights on.

SOLO: "Must Jesus Bear the Cross Alone?" (first verse)

READER: John 19:16-17

SCENE FOUR: Lights out. Set up the silhouette of the hill with three crosses. (See Fig. 5g.) Lights on.

CHOIR: "The Old Rugged Cross" (first verse, no chorus)

SOLO AND CHOIR: "There Is a Green Hill Far Away" (solo on first verse, choir on chorus)

44

Fig. 5*f*. Scene Three

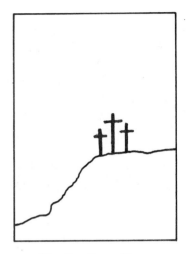

Fig. 5*g*. Scene Four

Fig. 5*h*. Scene Five

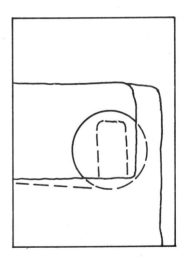

Fig. 5*i*. Scene Six

As the choir begins to sing the chorus, the colored wads appear and move back and forth to the beat of the music.

READER: Luke 15:24-34

Colored wads are still during the reading.

CHOIR: "The Old Rugged Cross" (second and third verses, no chorus)

Colored wads move slowly.

SCENE FIVE: *Lights out. Set up the cross outlined in black with red cellophane in its center. Lights on.*

SOLO: "When I Survey the Wondrous Cross"

On the last verse the colored wads move about at the foot of the cross. (See Fig. 5h.)

SCENE SIX: *Lights out. Set up the silhouette of the tomb, with door closed. (See Fig. 5i.) Lights on.*

CHOIR OR SOLO: "Low in the Grave He Lay" (three verses, no chorus)

At the end of the third verse, remove the door of the tomb. Bright yellow light shines from the tomb.

CHOIR: "Low in the Grave He Lay" (chorus only)

Colored cellophane wads move about joyously. During the last phrase of the chorus, the tomb is drawn away from the shadow screen so that it becomes very hazy and finally disappears.

SCENE SEVEN: *Nothing shows on the shadow screen except the cellophane wads moving about joyously.*

CHOIR: "Christ the Lord Is Risen Today"

6

Children's Day

A Puppet Play Using Black Light

NOTES FOR USE OF BLACK LIGHT

In recent years the use of ultraviolet light, called "black light," has become very popular. In some cultures in our society it has become the "thing to do" to use black light for special effects in the home. It is used for illuminating almost everything, from posters to furniture. But remember, ultraviolet light is not something that should be played with or used carelessly.

Never look directly into an ultraviolet light, because you could damage your sight. When using black light on a puppet stage, be sure that it is shielded from the audience's view, not only to enhance your puppet presentation but to protect the audience's eyes. *Never* allow children to experiment with ultraviolet light unless they have been properly trained in its use and you are *sure* that they will follow instructions. If you sit to present a puppet play, instead of being beneath the level of the stage, use sunglasses for your protection. *Do not* use plastic or Polaroid glasses. Use sunglasses of glass; they will give you the best protection. You will also find that the use of sunglasses even during ordinary lighted scenes will help you to see the stage and puppets better.

Several types of ultraviolet lights are available, ranging from small hand-held lights to large fluorescent-type rods. If you want to "black light" a small area such as a door, one tree, or one puppet that does not move far, then a small spot-light could be used. However, if you plan to use the black light for other performances (and you will, once you have tried it), then you should buy a black light that is shaped like a fluorescent-type tube and install it along the front and the bottom of your stage. (See Fig. 6a.) This type of black light has the same kind of fixtures that ordinary fluorescent lights have and comes with a movable shield for audience protection. *It must have this shield.*

In your puppet stories do not overdo the use of black light, because the value of a black-light scene is its shock effect. If it is overdone, then it rapidly loses its value.

Of course, black light cannot be used alone. It must be used with special paints that glow with the use of ultraviolet light. These can be purchased at almost any art store and at most stationery stores. They are inexpensive, so don't be afraid to experiment with them. Some of the paints are "invisible." That is, they might show up blue or another color under black light but will be white when seen with ordinary light. This will give you greater freedom in making your scenery.

In true-to-life stories you are rather limited in the use of black light except for such things as dream scenes, storms, hallucinations, fear (for example, "eyes" of animals when one is lost in the forest at night), and perhaps the appearance of an angel (in a Christmas story).

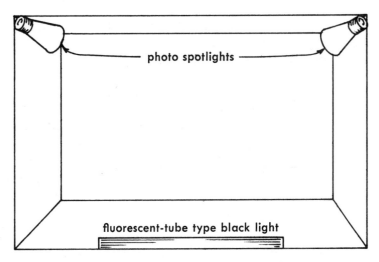

Fig. 6a. Lighting for use of black light

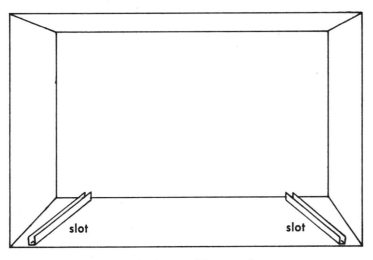

Fig. 6b. Stage with prop slots

49

In fantasy there is no limit. You could have illuminated trees, animals, buildings, or whatever would enhance the story you are presenting. The main thing to remember is not to overdo the black-light sequence. Always leave the audience with the feeling that they wish it had been longer, rather than not quite so long.

You can use the black-light paint along with poster paint or other types of paints. You can paint over water or oil colors so that your scenery will give the effect needed under utlraviolet light. The parts painted will glow under the black light, while the ones not painted with the special paint will not be seen. You do not have to be an artist to make the scenery and other props for your puppet plays. The idea is to convey an impression, not to give a detailed scene. Never let the complexity of your props distract from the puppets and their message.

LIGHTING

Your ordinary stage lights, which are not always necessary if the plays are presented in small, well-lighted rooms, can be photo spotlights attached to the top sides of the stage or on stands in front and on the sides of the puppet stage (see Fig. 6a).

They should be shielded so that the light does not shine into the audience's eyes. A dimmer switch is useful for controlling the amount of light.

You have to experiment to find which place is best for the lighting of your particular stage. You do not want bright spots on some puppets, and neither do you not want other puppets in the shadows.

We have found it advisable to make permanent slots on either side of our puppet stage (see Fig. 6*b*) in which to insert various scenery props. These props are made of heavy art cardboard which is available at art stores and many stationery stores. The props are painted to suggest either interiors or outdoor scenes. Our puppets can exit or enter from behind these props rather than pop up or disappear beneath the stage. In fantasy stories, such as "Punch and Judy," the character can pop up from below stage; but if you are trying to create a true-to-life scene, you would not have a puppet pop up through the floor!

The slots are two pieces of finely sanded wood fastened to the floor of the stage close enough together to allow the heavy cardboard prop to slip in easily and remain upright. The slots should be painted with *flat* black. Black is an "invisible" color and should always be used on controls for props, puppets, or marionettes. The flat black will not reflect the light from the spotlights and will not give unwanted bright spots on the stage, as white or any other color will. Black controls will not be seen by the audience.

The Three Little Pigs

CHARACTERS

PETER PIG: blue

PAULA PIG: pink

OLIVER PIG: green

WOLF: dark grey with long white fangs

NARRATOR

Costumes

PAULA: She should have two changes of costumes. The dress "like Suzi's" should be elaborate in decorations: beads, laces, frills, and any other decoration to make it ridiculous looking. The dress in Paula's final scene should be ragged, patched, and black or dirty white.

Props

PILLS: These may be made of thick cardboard and of exaggerated size. They can be held in the pigs' hands by bent pins sewed onto the discs. (See *You Can Be a Puppeteer,* p. 51.)

STONES: The stones that Oliver and Peter throw in the last scene should be large enough to be seen easily by the audience. They should be flat on one side so they will not roll off the stage. Do not use styrofoam as it is too light and too difficult to let loose. Any nonhardening modeling clay would make ideal stones.

BUILDINGS: These props should be made of heavy art cardboard. Keep the design simple. See Figs. 6c, 6d, 6e, 6f, 6g. Paula's house may be made from a straw placemat. The station, store, and school have smiling faces painted on with black-light paints (Fig. 6c). Paula's house (Fig. 6e) and Peter's house (Fig. 6f) have scowling faces painted on with black-light paints. These two houses should be mounted on rods to be shaken near end of play. Oliver's house (Fig. 6g) is painted to represent rock and has cross design on door.

(SCENE ONE: *The narrator stands beside the puppet stage. There are no props on the stage as the curtain opens. But as*

52

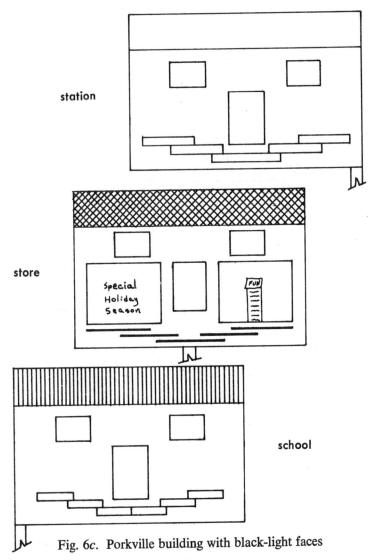

Fig. 6c. Porkville building with black-light faces

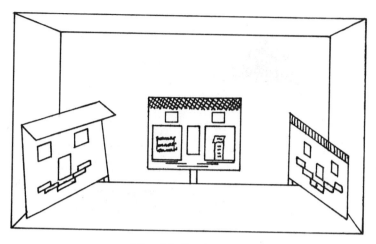

Fig. 6d. Scene One

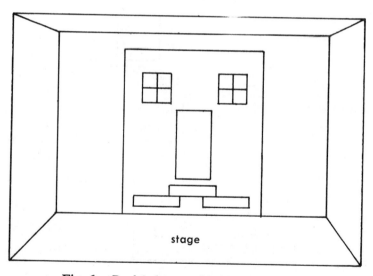

stage

Fig. 6e. Paula's house with black-light face

54

the narrator speaks, one by one the props pop up from below stage and are anchored in their appropriate places. See Fig. 6d.)

NARRATOR: Once upon a time, not so very long ago, there was a lovely little town called Porkville. Porkville was a happy town where all the little pigs lived and worked. Porkville had a busy railroad station *(place RR station),* because the town was on the commuter line between the large city of Here and the country village of There.

Then there was the grocery store *(place grocery),* a happy little store where all sorts of fruits and vegetables were sold. Of course, only *imitation* bacon was sold here. In the whole town of Porkville there was not one butcher shop.

And then there was the happy little school *(place school).* Baseball was the school's favorite sport, and of course there was no football. None of the players would like to kick a *pigskin!* The glee club was one of the best in the state and had some of the best oinkers and grunters anywhere. They often won blue ribbons for their singing. Their school spirit was very good, and no matter whether it was a baseball game or a glee club concert or a debating team contest, there were always a lot of *rooters* rooting for the home team.

(Turn spotlight off and black light on, revealing the smiling faces of the three props.)

NARRATOR: As I said, it was a very happy little town. On the side streets there were many happy homes where the pigs of Porkville all lived happily. *(Black light goes off, and spotlight begins to come on slowly—dim at first and*

55

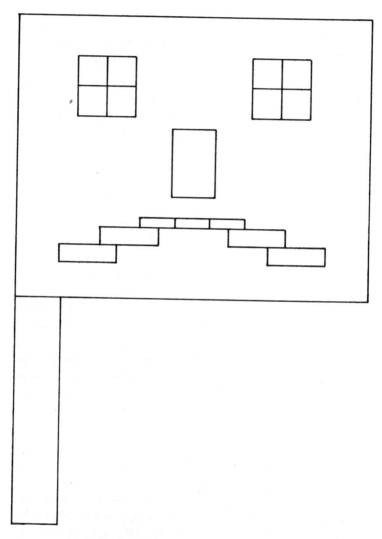

Fig. 6*f*. Peter's house with black-light face

56

Fig. 6g. Scene Five

then, by the time the narrator's speech is over, full bright-
ness.) That is, many of the pigs lived happily, most of the
time. Sometimes, though, some of them weren't quite as
happy as they should be. For instance, there was Peter
Pig. *(Peter Pig pops up near the RR station.)* Peter Pig
used to be happy, but lately he'd been neglecting his
studies.

PETER PIG: I've got a test today at school. Oh, wow! I
should have studied. I wish I'd studied harder. Now
I'm so worried and scared. I've got a lot of problems, too.
My life really isn't so happy anymore. I don't think

Mother Pig or Father Pig understand me anymore. I've got troubles at home and troubles with my friends, and now I'm going to have troubles at school. Oh, wow, have I got troubles! I've got troubles!

NARRATOR: And then—then there was Paula Pig. *(Paula appears.)*

PAULA PIG: Hi ya, Peter Pig! Hey, did you see that snazzy outfit Suzi Pig had on yesterday? I'm going to get one just like it. Everything Suzi does is "in." That's what I want to be—"in." If I do everything just like Suzi does—she's very popular, you know—then I will be popular, too. Being popular is the most important thing in the whole world. I want every pig in Porkville to like me. I even want you to like me, Peter Pig, even if you do have a scowl on your face, and your tail isn't as curly as it should be.

PETER PIG: Don't bother me with being liked! I've got my own worries. Oh, have I got worries! I wish I knew how to get rid of my worries. I didn't study, and I'm scared. I wish I knew how to get rid of being scared.

NARRATOR: And then—then there was Oliver Thomas Willam Jones Pig. *(Oliver pops up.)* Now, as you can imagine, Oliver Thomas William Jones Pig was a very independent type of pig. He had lots of friends. He was intelligent and very thoughtful and, well, why should *I* tell you about Oliver Thomas William Jones Pig? I'll let him talk for himself.

OLIVER: Hi, Peter! Hi, Paula! *(Whistles.)* It's a wallowing good day, now isn't it? Good enough day to curl your tail.

PETER: It's a terrible day! I've got a test. I've got troubles

58

at home. I've got all sorts of troubles and problems. I wish I had a trouble-solver.

PAULA: If you think you've got troubles, how about me? I want to be the most popular pig in all Porkville! I shall be the most popular, though! Just wait till I get an outfit like Suzi's!

PETER: Oh, quit your grunting! You don't know anything about troubles.

PAULA: Well, look who's talking! If you don't think it's hard trying to be the most popular pig in Porkville— It's really hard being like Suzi all the time.

OLIVER: You don't *have* to copy her, Paula. You'll be more popular if you will be friendly to pigs. You're not a copy cat; you're a *pig!*

PAULA: Oh, Oliver Thomas William Jones Pig, you just don't understand. You just don't understand what it is to be "in."

PETER: Oh, you both make me sick! Neither one of you knows what trouble is. Ugh, I've got a test. I know I'll flunk it. Oh, have I got problems. I wish I had a problem solver. Oh, have I got troubles! *(Exits.)*

PAULA: Huh! He thinks he's the only pig with problems. Why, just last night I called Suzi Pig, and she hung up on me! And I *do* want to be popular. I'm going to get a dress just like hers, and then she'll know how much I like her.

OLIVER: Paula, why don't you—

PAULA *(interrupting)*: There you go! You just know nothing about it at all! I've just *got* to be popular. The only way to have lots of friends is to do what every pig does. Follow the crowd, that's my motto. Well, Oliver Thomas William Jones Pig, it seems like you'll never learn. *(Exits.)*

(Oliver stares after her, shakes his head, and shrugs. Then he exits to the opposite side, whistling happily.)

NARRATOR: Little did Peter Pig, Paula Pig, and Oliver Thomas William Jones Pig realize the terrible thing that was about to happen. Wolf had moved into town! The big bad Wolf had appeared, and trouble was brewing for the three little Pigs!

(Curtain closes.)

(SCENE TWO: *Same as Scene One. If you have sound effects available, very solemn music could be played, or a few peals of thunder or the howling of a wolf. Many libraries carry sound-effect records to loan to the public. Curtain opens to the stage with all the previous buildings but no pigs. After a very brief interlude, Peter enters from one side and Oliver from the other. They meet in the middle of stage. Peter walks slowly with his head down and speaks with defiance; his conscience is hurting him. Oliver enters, whistling and happy.)*

OLIVER: Hello, Peter. I was wondering about you. This morning you said you had an examination at school. How did it go?

PETER: Oh, I didn't have to worry about it.

OLIVER: But, you were so worried. I don't understand. How is it that you suddenly didn't have to worry? Did the teacher cancel the examination? If so, you're all set. You can go home tonight and study.

PETER (*yawning*): I don't have to study.

OLIVER: Why? How did you get so smart, Peter?

PETER: Oliver Thomas William Jones Pig, you ask too many questions!

60

OLIVER: Oink! I—I just wanted to know how you were getting on with your studies. I'm your friend.

PETER: I've got a new friend. Did you meet the new arrival?

OLIVER: You mean *Wolf?* I heard he had moved into town.

PETER: Yep, Wolf has moved to Porkville.

OLIVER: I saw him, and I avoided him. Peter, do you know that Wolf has opened a butcher shop? He's opened a butcher shop in Porkville!

PETER: I met Wolf this morning when I was walking to school. We got to talking, and I told him I needed a problem-solver. And he had one!

OLIVER: You'd better leave him alone. He's bad news!

PETER: He's a nice guy.

OLIVER: He's *not* a nice guy! He's the big bad Wolf, and I'm avoiding him.

PETER: Wolf helped me. He gave me a pill, and I didn't worry about my examination. It was a good problem-solver!

OLIVER: A *pill?*

PETER: (*yawning*): Yes, a downer, or something like that he called it. I swallowed it, and pretty soon I wasn't worried about the test at all. I wasn't—

OLIVER: Did you pass the test?

PETER: I don't think so, but I don't care. I think I'll go home now and sleep. I'm not worried—

OLIVER: But, we've got a baseball game!

PETER (*yawning*): I don't care. I think I'll sleep. Yes, Wolf's OK. He's got all the answers—answers to worrying about examinations.

OLIVER: Did he tell you to study?

PETER: He's got the best problem-solver ever, the answer

to any worry. Just pop a pill and *pow!* The worries are gone! I guess I'd better go get more pills; I've got lots of problems.

OLIVER: See! Wolf hasn't gotten rid of your problems for you. You've still got them!

PETER: I'm going to find him.

(Oliver tries to stop him. He hangs onto Peter, and Peter shouts and struggles.)

PETER: Let me go! I've got to get rid of my problems! *(Finally breaks away and exits.)*

OLIVER *(shakes his head sadly and walks up and down stage muttering to himself)*: Poor Peter. Poor Peter.

(Paula enters.)

PAULA: Oliver Thomas William Jones Pig, look what I've got. I've got a new dress just like Suzi's. And look, I've got something else. *(Holds out her hand in which a large, oversize pill is plainly visible.)*

OLIVER: Where did you get that? That's dangerous! I've just got to do something to get rid of that Wolf. He's dangerous. He's no good. Oh, Paula, throw it away!

PAULA: I got the dress at Hog's Department Store, and I got the pill—my "make-me-happy pill"—from my new friend, Wolf! I'm happy!

OLIVER: Throw that away! It's dangerous!

PAULA: Oh, don't be a prig! You're a pig, not a prig! It makes me feel happy and peppy and everyone loves me, and it's groovy!

OLIVER: It's not groovy. It's gory, and you'll wind up in the sausage grinder!

PAULA: A stick-in-the-mud pig, that's what you are. Wolf's my friend.

OLIVER: He's not a friend, he's a fiend. He's decayed, defective, and deplorable. He's disgusting, dreadful, dire, rank, and foul. He's rotten and repelling and repulsive. He's defective and deplorable—

PAULA: You said that already.

OLIVER: Stay away from Wolf. He's bad!

PAULA: I know what I'm doing. He might be dangerous to some pigs, but not to me. When I get tired of playing with Wolf, I'll stop.

OLIVER: He'll come after you!

PAULA: I'll get into my house and lock the door, then he can't hurt me. I know what I'm doing.

OLIVER: Paula, I wish you'd move out of that straw house.

PAULA: Straw houses are popular this year. Everyone's living in straw houses.

OLIVER: But in trouble, or a storm—

PAULA: Who's going to have trouble or a storm? I'm happy! Whee! I'm happy! I took one make-me-happy pill this afternoon, and now I'm going to take this one. *(Makes motion as though to take the pill.)*

(Oliver rushes over and knocks pill from hand.)

PAULA *(begins to cry)*: You've knocked my pretty pill out of my hand. Help me find it. *(Begins to run around frantically looking for pill.)* You just don't want me to be happy!

OLIVER: You don't sound very happy. Wolf will kill you!

PAULA: My straw house will keep him out *when* I want him out! *(Looks for pill.)* Oh, where is my make-me-happy pill? Where is my make-me-happy pill? Oh, there it is! *(Swallows it quickly before Oliver can get it away from*

63

her.) Now I'll be happy. *(Exits while talking.)* Now I'll be happy and popular, and everyone will like me.

(Enter Peter with a large pill in his hand.)

PETER: I've got it! I've got my "don't-worry-anymore pill."

OLIVER *(rushes over and knocks it out of his hand)*: That's dangerous!

(Peter hits Oliver. Oliver tries to ward off the blow but doesn't hit back.)

PETER: You! You knocked my don't-worry pill out of my hand! Now I'm worried that I won't be able to find it. *(Rushes around looking for it.)* I just went to Wolf, and he gave me one to take so I wouldn't worry, and look what you did!

OLIVER: Wolf is dangerous. He'll kill you!

PETER: I know what I'm doing. I'll just take his pills until I stop worrying. He won't get me. When I am through with his pills, I'll just go into my house and lock the door.

OLIVER: Peter, you know that house of yours won't stand any *breeze,* let alone Wolf pounding on it.

PETER: Oliver Thomas William Jones Pig, you know my house is a very nice wooden house. I've gotten the wood from all over the world. *(Stops looking for pill and talks.)* I know what I'm doing. When I'm through with Wolf, I'll close the door.

OLIVER: Your house is just a shack. It will fall down! You got your wood down at the dump. That's where you got your wood.

PETER: I've got wood in my house from India and China and Japan and Africa. I've got glass windows from England. Of course, they are a bit scratched up; and when you look through them, you can't see out very well. But

it's a good house and I like it. The wood in my house
came from all over the world!

OLIVER: Yes, but sensible pigs threw that wood out a long
time ago. Your wooden house will fall down.

PETER: *(looking for pill again)*: Oh, stop talking. You
make me nervous.

OLIVER: What you need is a strong house built of *rock* and
built on *rock*.

PETER: You make me nervous. Now, where is my don't-
worry-anymore pill? Oh! There it is. *(Jumps for it before Oliver can take it away from him and swallows it.)*
Now I'm going home and not worry.

(Curtain closes.)

NARRATOR: We're going to see what happens to Peter and
Paula and Oliver Thomas William Jones Pig in just a mo-
ment. I think they are in trouble, don't you? Of course,
Oliver doesn't seem to be in any trouble, because he's not
listening to Wolf and his lies. But, poor Paula and Peter!
You know, in the Bible we read about a house on the
Rock (reads Matthew 7:24-27).

DISCUSSION

The narrator should lead the children in a discussion of
just what is meant by Jesus' words in Matthew 7:24-27.
Such questions as the following may be asked the children,
discussed, and explained:

1. Have you ever seen a flood?
2. When a bad storm comes, what happens to houses that
   aren't built properly?
3. Do you think that Jesus was only talking about actual

houses, or do you think He had something else in mind also?

4. What did He mean when He talked about lives being built on rock?
5. Who has a life "built on sand"?
6. Who has a life "built on rock"?
7. Who is "the Rock"?

Then the narrator should lead the children into a discussion of just what Paula's straw house and Peter's wooden house might mean. Lead the children into the idea that the straw house might mean following the fashions and plans of the world and Peter's wooden house could mean following the religions of the world. In this present age, when so much thought is given to Oriental philosophies and religions, it is good to get the children thinking about the falseness of these beliefs and their inability to help in time of trouble.

The discussion should be kept to the point and ended within seven or eight minutes. Do not preach or belabor the point. Ask leading questions and give help with the answers when needed.

* * *

NARRATOR: We've been talking about these houses that Paula and Peter built. Now let's go see Paula's house.
(Curtain closes.)

(SCENE THREE: *Paula's house is shown. Paula enters, wearing ragged dress.*)

PAULA (*crying*): Oh, I'm so unhappy. Nobody—nobody loves me. *(Paula's speech is confused, and she makes frequent inversions of syllables.)* I hurt. My head aches.

I'm scared and my hands are shaking. And I can't get any more money to buy—nomey to puy—money to buy—buy Wolf's pills. Everyone's against me. Nobody loves me.

(Enter Oliver, whistling. He walks in a short way and stops whistling when he sees Paula.)

OLIVER: Why, Paula! Where have you been? Your friends have been so worried about you. We haven't seen you in weeks!

PAULA: Go away! I don't have any friends. You're against me. Every pig is against me. No pig loves me. Every pig hates me. I don't have any friends.

OLIVER: Paula, you're confused.

PAULA: I don't have any money to buy Wolf's pills. I sold all my clothes, and now I'm in rags. I hurt and I'm scared.

OLIVER: Stop playing with Wolf.

PAULA: I want to, but I'm scared! I'm shaky.

OLIVER: Your friends will help you.

PAULA: I don't have any friends. I'm going into my house and shut the door, and Wolf can't hurt me, and you can't get me. I don't trust any pig! I don't have any friends.

OLIVER: Oh, Paula, you need a house built out of rock. Your house won't stand up.

PAULA *(enters house)*: Go away! I don't have any friends. Oh, I hurt. I'm scared.

(Oliver walks away, shaking his head and moving slowly as though worried. As he leaves one side of the stage, Wolf enters.)

WOLF *(with very sugary voice)*: Paula! Paula! It's your friend Wolf. *(Lights begin to dim. Paula doesn't appear, but her voice is heard.)*

67

PAULA: I hurt. Oh, I hurt! Give me one of your pills to make me stop hurting.

WOLF: Give me some money, Paula.

PAULA: I haven't any money. I'm scared and I hurt. Oh, I'm scared. I hurt. Give me some of your pills. No, go away! I don't want any of your pills. I don't want your pills. Go away!

WOLF: Give me some money, Paula, and I'll give you nice pillie-pill to make your hurt go way!

(Now spotlights are out, and black light comes on, revealing Paula's house to have sneer on face.)

PAULA: I'm scared! I'm scared! *(Screams.)*

WOLF: Let me in, little piggy. Let me come in.

PAULA: No, not by the hair of my chinny chin chin, I won't let you come in!

WOLF: Then I'll huff and I'll puff and I'll blow your house down!

PAULA: You can't blow my house down. I won't let you come in, not by the hair of my chinny chin chin. You can't come in!

(Wolf begins to huff and puff; house begins to shake.)

PAULA *(screams)*: I'm so scared. Help! Help!

(The house shakes violently as Wolf continues to huff and puff. Finally Wolf gives a leap, Paula screams, and house and Wolf disappear beneath stage. Black light goes out. Curtain closes.)

(SCENE FOUR: *Peter's wooden house is shown. Peter enters.*)

PETER: I'd better take another pill. Paula's disappeared. I haven't seen her for three days. *(Searches pockets, finds pill, swallows it. This is done by pantomime; no pill is used in this scene.)* There, now I'll feel better. Maybe I'll quit worrying. I think—I'm sure that Wolf must have eaten Paula, and I've got a notion that he's going to try to eat me, too.

(Enter Oliver, whistling.)

OLIVER: Hello, Peter. It's a beautiful day.

PETER: Oliver Thomas William Jones Pig, this is a worrying day!

OLIVER: I thought you'd solved the problem about worrying.

PETER: Oh, Oliver Thomas William Jones Pig, the more pills I take to stop worrying, the more worrying I do about whether or not I'll have enough pills to stop worrying! And I'm worried. Paula's disappeared. I haven't seen her for three days. I think Wolf ate her!

OLIVER: Poor Paula! I warned her. I tried to stop her from playing with Wolf.

PETER: I guess she wasn't smart enough. Now, me, I'm too smart for Wolf. He'll never get me. He'll never eat me. I'm too smart for him. *(Moves to front of his house and "whispers" to audience.)* I'm not going to let Oliver Thomas William Jones know that I am really scared to death of Wolf. *(Turns back to Oliver.)* Now, when I get tired of playing with Wolf, I'll just go into my house—like this *(enters house)*—and close the door *(voice comes from inside),* and Wolf will never get me.

OLIVER: Peter, come home with me. My rock house is big enough for many pigs! Come with me, and you'll be safe from Wolf.

PETER: Go away!

(Oliver leaves, shaking his head and calling back.)

OLIVER: When you need some help, remember you are safe at the rock house. Come live with me.

(Enter Wolf.)

WOLF *(angrily)*: Peter! Peter, come out and let me eat you!

PETER: Is that you, Wolf?

WOLF: Of course. I'm not going to waste any time. Come out and let me eat you!

PETER: Don't be silly. I'm safe in my house. I don't think you are very nice. I'm not going to let you eat me. *(Speaks with worried voice now.)* You really aren't going to eat me, are you?

WOLF: Come out! Come out and find out!

PETER: I'm safe in my wooden house. I don't think I'll come out and try anything foolish.

WOLF: You've already been foolish. There is no way you can escape me now! I'll huff and I'll puff and I'll blow your house down. *(Begins to huff and puff. Black light goes on, and spotlight dims.)*

PETER: I won't let you in. Not by the hair of my chinny chin chin, I won't let you in!

WOLF *(huffing and puffing)*: I'll blow your house down.

(House shakes violently. Peter screams.)

PETER: What was that Oliver said? I remember, I remember! Oh, my house! My house is falling down. I've got to hurry.

WOLF: I'll huff and I'll puff. *(Lunges. House collapses, and Wolf and house disappear beneath stage.)*

(SCENE FIVE: Oliver's rock house is on stage. Lights are up to full brightness. Wolf enters.)

70

WOLF: Grr! Grr! I'm hungry and I'm angry. I'm hungry. I blew Peter's wooden house down, and I couldn't find him. All I got was a splinter in my nose! He escaped me. He escaped me! I'm so hungry. Hm, I've never been able to blow a rock house down, but I'm going to have to *try. (Voice becomes sugary.)* Oliver Thomas William Jones Pig, are you home?

(Oliver's head pops up over roof of rock house.)

OLIVER: Not to you, Wolf, I'm not home to huffing and puffing wolves.

WOLF: Why, Oliver Thomas William Jones Pig, I have never huffed or puffed in my life!

PETER *(head pops up above rock house)*: Oh, is that so, Mr. Huffing and Puffing Wolf?

WOLF: Curse you, Peter Pig! I'm hungry!

PETER: I escaped from my wooden house, and now I'm safe in the house of rock!

WOLF *(sugary voice)*: I've got something that will make you stop worrying, Peter .

PETER: I *have* stopped worrying! I'm safe in the house of rock!

WOLF *(angrily)*: Come out and let me eat you both.

PETER: No, we're safe now.

WOLF: I'll huff and I'll puff and I'll blow your house down!

OLIVER: You can't blow a house of rock down!

WOLF *(huffing and puffing)*: I'll blow your house down. I'll huff and I'll puff and I'll blow your house down!

(Wolf starts to huff and puff, but the house doesn't shake. Peter and Oliver start dropping stones onto Wolf's head. Wolf howls and tries to dodge them, but the pigs keep dropping them on his head. He huffs and puffs and finally col-

lapses, exhausted, on the stage while the stones drop on him.
Defeated, he crawls off stage, howling and rubbing his head.
As he leaves, he speaks.)

WOLF: I can't get into that house. I'll have to go somewhere else. Oh, my head hurts! Oh, my back hurts! I'm so hungry, and I hurt *(howls).*

(Peter and Oliver are still throwing stones at him and laughing as Wolf exits.)

(Curtain closes.)

7

Day of Prayer

Elijah and the Priests of Baal

CHARACTERS

FIRST MAN	OBADIAH
SECOND MAN	KING AHAB
ELIJAH	MEN OF ISRAEL
SERVANT	PROPHETS OF BAAL

ROD PUPPETS: The Men of Israel and the Prophets of Baal are to be attached to controlling rods. (See Fig. 7a.) There should be a hook in the back of one of the puppets of the Men of Israel so they can be hooked to the back curtain (or they can be stuck in a holder on the shelf beneath the stage). The Men of Israel and the Prophets of Baal are two groups, each on a rod, and may be simply puppet heads with pieces of cloth to represent robes. The heads should be of styrofoam to be as lightweight as possible. They may have beards of dark yarn and turbans or hoods. The robes of the Prophets of Baal should be light colored so the red yarn "blood" will show up well. Their clothing should be distinctive from the Men of Israel.

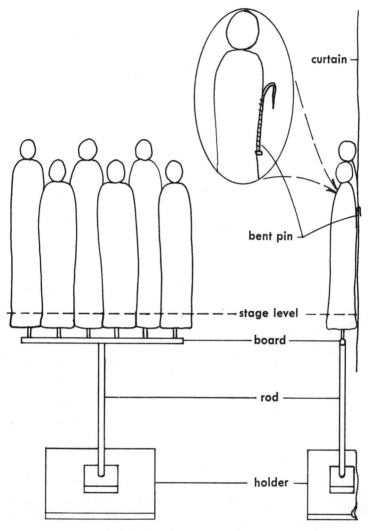

Fig. 7a. Rod puppets

74

BACKDROP: This should be bright yellow to represent a hot sky.

SUN: This should be bright yellow, outlined with red, and attached to a control rod. (See Fig. 7*b*.)

TWO HOES: These are for Elijah and Servant.

LONG KNIFE OR SWORD: This is for Elijah.

STICKS OF WOOD FOR ALTARS

RED YARN OR RIBBON: Pieces of yarn or ribbon represent blood and should be prepared so it will stick quickly to the robes of the Prophets of Baal.

TWO BULLOCK CARCASSES: These may be modeled out of clay or of papier-maché.

CAMERA WITH FLASHBULB: This should not be an electronic flash.

FOUR FILLED WATER BARRELS: These may be plastic caps painted brown. They must be large enough to be carried by the Servant and seen by the audience.

BAAL'S ALTAR

JEHOVAH'S ALTAR: This may be made on a wide-mouth jar lid, such as one from a large mayonnaise or pickle jar. Turn the lid upside down, and on the side facing the audience, attach three or four stones either of wads of dark gray paper, modeling clay, or papier-maché. (See Fig. 7*c*.) Have enough stones lying on stage to complete the twelve required for script. Inside the upturned lid, close to the front edge, glue a stryofoam base or stick some modeling clay to help support the rest of the stones when Elijah rebuilds the altar. Measure the water so you have enough to almost fill the mayonnaise lid. (If it splashes over, there will be no damage.) If you want to have a very spectacu-

red outline

wire rod

Fig. 7b. Sun

76

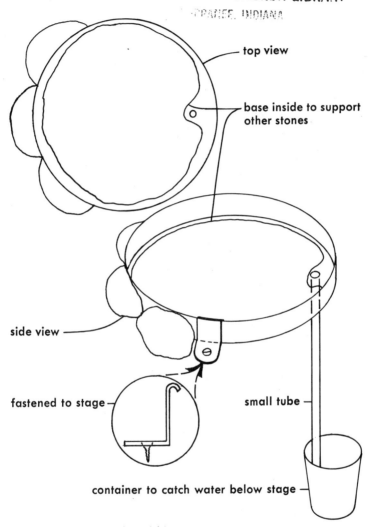

top view

base inside to support
other stones

side view

fastened to stage

small tube

container to catch water below stage

Fig. 7c. Jehovah's altar

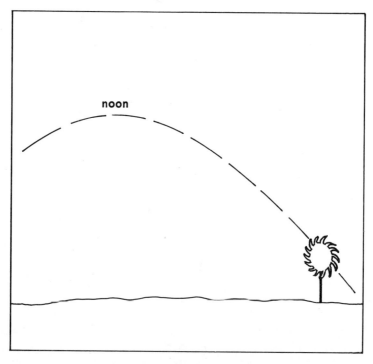

Fig. 7d. Movement of sun during day

lar water scene, you could attach a small tube or even a plastic drinking straw and have this drain off into a container below stage. If you do this, then you can have very large containers of water brought in and poured on the offering.

(SCENE ONE: *Stage is empty. Bright yellow backdrop is in place, and sun is at low "east" side. See Fig. 7h. Enter First Man and Second Man. The purpose of these two pup-*

pets and their conversation is to set the scene and give the audience a bit of background for the story.)

FIRST MAN: Eh, it is so early in the morning, and yet look *(points to sun).* It burns like fire.

SECOND MAN: Eh, I think that the sun will dry up my very bones. It has been three years now since rain has fallen on Israel.

FIRST MAN: It is all the fault of that prophet Elijah. It is his fault. The prophet Elijah called down this curse upon our land.

SECOND MAN: *(bends over and searches the ground)*: I am hoping to find a seed or a dried weed to eat. But there is nothing!

FIRST MAN: I have a cousin who is a servant in the house of King Ahab. He was there sweeping the floor, unnoticed in the corner, when the prophet Elijah came in to see King Ahab.

SECOND MAN: I would like to see this prophet Elijah; he is a great and fearless man. *(Straightens up and moves around looking for seed on ground.)*

FIRST MAN: Eh! It is his fault that you are hungry. My cousin said that he heard the prophet tell King Ahab that the Lord God of Israel would send no rain or dew except by Elijah's word. Who is he that he thinks Jehovah will listen only to his word? Yes, it is the prophet's fault that we suffer so greatly.

SECOND MAN: But don't you see? The Lord Jehovah *has* listened to the prophet. Sometimes I think that it is not Elijah's fault that we have no rain. We have left the true worship that we learned from our forefathers. We have followed King Ahab and the worship of Baal. Perhaps

79

it is true that Jehovah is angry with us. Perhaps we should repent and turn back to Him. I should greatly like to see this prophet Elijah!

FIRST MAN: Hush! You never know when Ahab's spies will be around.

SECOND MAN (*looking around and pointing*): And where would they hide in this barren land? There is not even a blade of grass left! My children are hungry.

FIRST MAN: We are all hungry, and we are tired of this sun. But if you voice words of approval of the prophet Elijah, then King Ahab will search you out and kill you. He has been looking for Elijah for many days, my cousin tells me.

SECOND MAN: We should repent and return to the worship of Jehovah. But, like you, I fear King Ahab. *(Bends down and picks up something.)* Ah, here is one tiny seed. *(Puts it in his mouth.)* I do not know Baal or Jehovah. All I know is that some god—either Baal or Jehovah—should answer our prayers and send us rain.

FIRST MAN: I have heard that a servant in the house of King Ahab is very friendly toward the prophets of Jehovah. But King Ahab does not know about this man.

SECOND MAN: If there is such a man, then surely he is in a very dangerous position, for King Ahab will have his head. If King Ahab knew that one of his servants was friendly toward the prophets of Jehovah, he would kill him quickly.

FIRST MAN: I do not know if it is true or not, but I have heard that it is the man called Obadiah.

SECOND MAN: Obadiah! Why, Obadiah is one of the most important men in King Ahab's palace! Obadiah is in charge of the king's household. Eh, that would be strange to have Obadiah, one of the most important servants to King Ahab, friendly to the men who follow Jehovah.

FIRST MAN: Well, I don't know; but if Baal is powerful, he surely must answer the prayers of the priests and King Ahab and send us rain.

SECOND MAN: Eh, the sun is so hot, I think I shall surely die. I will go rest for a while.

(They exit. Enter Elijah and his servant from one side.)

SERVANT: Elijah, my master, it is very dangerous for you to make this trip. If King Ahab sees you, then he will surely kill you. Let us return—

ELIJAH: It is to see King Ahab that I have come. It is time to show the king that his wickedness and sin are not ignored by Jehovah.

(Enter Obadiah from opposite side.)

SERVANT: But, Master Elijah, he has his spies looking for you to kill you.

ELIJAH: I will see King Ahab. *(He sees Obadiah, and Obadiah recognizes him. Obadiah runs toward Elijah and bows to the ground.)*

OBADIAH: Sir! Are you the prophet Elijah? Are you Elijah?

ELIJAH: I am. I am Elijah, the prophet of the Lord Jehovah.

SERVANT *(tugging on Elijah's sleeve)*: Please, sir, don't tell him who you are! It is dangerous!

ELIJAH *(pointing to Obadiah)*: You are Obadiah. *(Elijah raises Obadiah to standing position.)* You are the servant of King Ahab. I want you to go to your master, the wicked king, and tell him that Elijah is here.

OBADIAH: Oh, sir. Oh, great prophet Elijah, would you have me killed? Surely if I go to King Ahab and tell him that you are here, and he comes searching for you, the Spirit of Jehovah will catch you away. Then King Ahab's wrath will be poured out on me. Already I have risked my head for Jehovah and His servants. I have hid one hundred of the prophets of Jehovah, and I have fed them with food from King Ahab's house. I have risked my life. Now, sir, would you have me killed?

SERVANT: Please, Master Elijah, let's get out of here and leave this good man alone in peace!

ELIJAH: Obadiah, go tell King Ahab that the servant of the living God will see him. Tell King Ahab that Elijah, the prophet of the Lord Jehovah, will see him. I will not hide, nor will the Spirit of Jehovah carry me away. I will see King Ahab and prove to him that Jehovah liveth.

OBADIAH: Oh, sir, don't you know that King Ahab hates you? He has searched everywhere on the face of this earth looking for you!

ELIJAH: I promise you that I will see King Ahab. Go tell him that the prophet of Jehovah, Elijah, is coming to see him this day.

OBADIAH (*bowing*): Yes, yes, my lord, I will tell him. *(Leaves the stage by the same side that he entered.)*

SERVANT: Oh, my master, I fear for our lives. King Ahab will surely kill us.

ELIJAH: Today I will face King Ahab, and he will know that Jehovah is the living God.

(Enter Ahab from same side that Obadiah exited.)

KING: So! *It is you!* Aren't you the one who has been troubling Israel? You are the one who has brought all this trouble on this land. I've looked everywhere for you, and now I've found you.

ELIJAH: It is not I, Ahab, but *you* who has troubled this

land. You are the one who has forsaken the command-
ments of the Lord Jehovah, and you have followed the
false god, Baal.

AHAB: I should kill you now! I should kill you now!

(Servant trembles and falls to the ground.)

ELIJAH: I have not troubled the land. Now I will prove to
you that Jehovah is the God to fear and worship. Go, call
your false prophets of Baal, those 450 men who are false
prophets of Baal. Go, call the ones who care for the
wicked places of worship of Baal. Go, King Ahab, and
call them together. I will prove to you that Jehovah lives
and hears my prayers.

AHAB: I will gather them at Mount Carmel. They will prove
to you that it is not Jehovah but Baal, who hears and answers prayer.

ELIJAH: Ahab, Jehovah is angry. Today you will know that
Jehovah is God!

(Curtain closes.)

(SCENE TWO: *Yellow backdrop remains in place. Sun has
moved slightly westward but not very far. On the stage are
all the props necessary for the scene, except the water barrels
and the yarn. The yarn for the blood should be easily available below stage. Fasten altar securely to stage. The Men of
Israel are hooked to the back curtain. See Figure 7e for stage
setting. All characters, including King Ahab, are on stage at
curtain.*)

ELIJAH (*pointing to Men of Israel*): Men of Israel, listen to
me! How long will you stand between two opinions? Don't
you know that Jehovah is God? If you think Baal is the

83

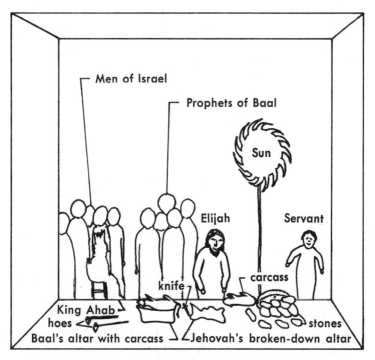

Fig. 7e. Scene Two

one who is god, then follow him. But if it is Jehovah who is God, then follow Jehovah.

Now, you prophets and followers of Baal *(points to them),* let's see what Baal can do. Let's see if Baal can answer prayer. We have two bulls here. You killed one, and I killed one. Let us see if Baal will answer you. Let us see if Baal will send fire from heaven and burn your offering.

Go on! Start calling on your god, Baal, and let's see if he will answer you.

84

(Baal's prophets start dancing and shouting and moving around. This is done by merely moving the rod up and down. Occasionally bring the rod up and toward the rear so that the prophets will seem to bow.)

PROPHETS *(shouting)*: Baal, Baal, listen to us. Hear us. We have an offering for you. Baal, hear us!

ELIJAH: Ho hum! I think it's too early in the morning for Baal to hear you. I think he's still asleep. You'd better wake him up. Shout louder!

PROPHET: Baal, hear us! *(Continue shouting.)*

ELIJAH: Go on, tell Baal you've got a good offering for him.

PROPHETS *(shouting)*: Hear us (etc.)!

SERVANT *(pulls on Elijah's sleeve)*: Master, don't make them angry. They may harm us.

ELIJAH: Go on, tell Baal you're waiting for him.

(The sun moves very slowly toward "noon" center of back-stage curtain during this shouting. See Fig. 7d. The scene may be ad-libbed, with the prophets screaming to Baal and Elijah taunting them. When the sun is exactly center, Elijah speaks again.) ·

ELIJAH: We've been here since early morning and still your Baal has not heard you. Cry aloud, for surely Baal is a real god. If he really is able to hear you, then he must be talking so loudly that he can't hear you. *(Prophets shout.)* Well, maybe he's out running around somewhere. Yes, that's the case; he's out running around.

SERVANT *(to Elijah)*: Master, I'm almost beginning to enjoy this. I think maybe Baal must be out looking for a drink of water!

ELIJAH: *(shouting to the prophets)*: Perhaps Baal's on a journey!

85

SERVANT: I think he's gone somewhere where it's nice and cool!

(Prophets continue shouting and dancing. They bow down, and the puppeteer quickly attaches the yarn.)

ELIJAH: Look! The servants of Baal are even cutting themselves so that Baal will notice them. Blood is pouring from them, and still their god does not hear them.

SERVANT: Master! They have used knives on their bodies to bring blood!

ELIJAH: It is noon. The sun is standing overhead, and still your god has not come to your aid! Shout louder! Cut yourselves deeper! Cry to him, he's asleep! *(Continues.)*

(The prophets dance and shout as the sun moves toward the "west." As it reaches its late afternoon position, Elijah commands the prophets of Baal to stop and listen.)

ELIJAH: Stop! I have something to say. You have danced and shouted and cut yourselves, and there is no answer. Baal has not paid any attention to you. It is now the time of the evening sacrifice. Now, behold! Watch! See what will happen.

ELIJAH *(pointing to servant)*: Let us repair the altar of Jehovah. Gather up twelve stones. *(They pick up the stones and place them on the altar base.)* Now dig a trench around the altar.

SERVANT: A trench, sir? Why?

ELIJAH: Help me dig a trench. *(They pick up hoes and dig for a few seconds.)*

ELIJAH: Now bring wood.

(The servant picks up wood and lays it on the altar.)

ELIJAH: Now bring the bullock.

(Elijah and servant pick up the bullock. Elijah picks up sword or long knife and hacks at the offering.)

ELIJAH: Go, bring some water. Bring four barrels of water. *(Servant goes off stage and returns with a barrel of real water in his arms. Elijah takes it and pours it over the offering.)*

SERVANT: Oh, Master Elijah, do not make things too difficult for the Lord Jehovah!

ELIJAH: Go, bring more water.

(Servant returns for water; he makes three trips. Each time Elijah pours the water over the offering.)

SERVANT: Oh, Master Elijah, what are you doing? This is too much! You are making this impossible for the Lord Jehovah! Stop, please, master! Oh, Master Elijah, you are making this impossible!

ELIJAH (*bows and prays*): O Lord God of Abraham, Isaac, and of Israel, let it be known this day that Thou art God in Israel and that I am Thy servant, and that I have done all these things at Thy word.

Hear me, O Lord, hear me, that this people may know that Thou art the Lord God and that Thou hast turned their heart back again.

(As Elijah is about to finish his prayer, one of the puppeteers slips a camera with flashbulb up to the altar. At the last phrase of Elijah's prayer the flashbulb is pushed up just above the level of the bullock. At the end of the prayer, the bulb is flashed. Immediately the altar is pulled off the stage. This must be done at the instant the bulb is flashed.)

PROPHETS OF BAAL AND MEN OF ISRAEL (*in unison and bowing*): The Lord Jehovah, He is God. The Lord, He is God.

ELIJAH: Men of Israel *(points to them)*, take the prophets of Baal. Let not one of them escape.

(The men of Israel move quickly to the prophets of Baal; and pressed close together, both prophets and Men of Israel are removed from stage.)

(Curtain closes.)

(SCENE THREE: *This is same as Scene One, but there is no sun. Second Man is on stage.)*

FIRST MAN *(entering)*: Ah, greetings, friend.

SECOND MAN: Greetings, I greet you in the name of the one and only true God, the Lord Jehovah.

FIRST MAN: Truly the Lord Jehovah is God. Yesterday the Lord Jehovah answered the prayer of the prophet Elijah.

SECOND MAN: And all the wicked priests of Baal are dead.

FIRST MAN: The Lord Jehovah sent much rain yesterday.

SECOND MAN: Ah, it was a good rain. And my heart has been refreshed not only with the rain but with the knowledge that the Lord God Jehovah does hear and answer prayer.

FIRST MAN: And my heart, also. I have returned to the true worship of the true God, the Lord Jehovah.

SECOND MAN: Come, let us go give thanks unto Jehovah, for He is good.

FIRST MAN: The eyes of the Lord are upon the righteous, and His ears are open unto their cry.

(They exit. Curtain closes.)

8

African Missionary Play

GRANDSON: young boy
GRANDFATHER: elderly man
SHOLA: Grandfather as a boy
OLU: young boy
MEDICINE MAN

All the puppets are black Africans. Only two puppeteers are needed if the play is recorded beforehand. However, if the stage is large enough, five puppeteers could be used.

COSTUMES

GRANDSON: He is dressed in white shirt with blue bottom to represent school pants. He may have a small white cap on his head.

GRANDFATHER: He is dressed in a long light-colored robe. He may have a small cap on head and have a short grey beard.

MEDICINE MAN: His face should be painted with wild colors

view of houses

staples

prop

back view of houses

stage

Fig. 8a. Village scene

90

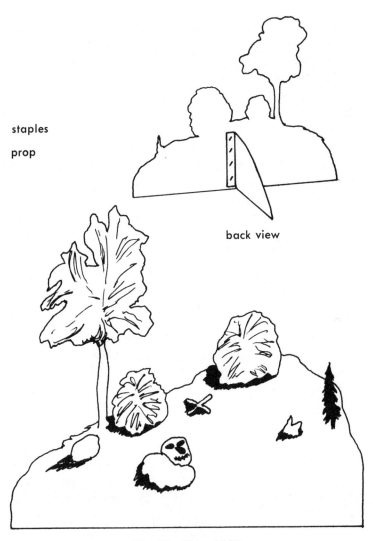

staples

prop

back view

Fig. 8b. Sacred hill

91

and designs. He has bones and small ornaments around his neck. His clothing is mostly rags hung on his body. His hair is disheveled, with sticks and bones in it.

SHOLA: His robe should be light colored and leave one shoulder uncovered.

OLU: His robe should be brightly colored.

PROPS

TOY TOP: This should be small enough for Grandson to carry in his hand.

VILLAGE SCENE: See Figure 8*a*.

SACRED HILL: See Figure 8*b*. Black light is not necessary for the hill-climbing scene, but it will add to the eeriness of the situation. The hill may be painted with a few crossbones and skulls, and some of the bushes may be outlined with black-light paint.

(SCENE ONE: *Grandfather and Grandson on stage. No scenery is needed. The back curtain should be of a contrasting color, very light so that the puppets' dark faces and bodies show up against it. Grandson plays with top as curtain opens.*)

GRANDFATHER: How was school today, Grandson?

GRANDSON (*sadly*): It was OK, Grandfather.

GRANDFATHER: You do not sound very happy. Your face does not shine with joy. Your grandfather likes to see your face with joy.

GRANDSON: Garba tried to take my top away from me. I worked hard making it, and he wanted it. And besides, he's always making fun of me for being a Christian. He said that I only went to church because my mother made me go. He said that I was weak and cowardly, and he called me selfish. Grandfather Shola, he hurt my feelings!

GRANDFATHER: And what did you tell him?

GRANDSON: Ap! I told him it was my top, and he couldn't have it. And—and then—then I ran away. Grandfather Shola, I ran and hid.

GRANDFATHER: Did you invite him to go to church with you?

GRANDSON: That would only make matters worse. He's always teasing me, and it's embarrassing. I just don't like it. I shall never tell anyone again that I'm a Christian.

GRANDFATHER: That is a pity! When I think how the Lord Jesus loves you—and Garba—so much. I should think everyone would want to talk about Jesus.

GRANDSON: You don't know what it is like to have people make fun of you. When you were young, things were different. A long time ago it was all different. You didn't have troubles. It was different then, very different. Grandfather, it's all right for you to say people should tell others about the Lord Jesus. You just don't know what it is to suffer. Why, it's terrible having people make fun of me because I tell them I'm a Christian or they see me going to church. No, I'm never going to tell anyone about the Lord Jesus. You just don't know what it means having to be teased for Jesus.

GRANDFATHER: Perhaps I don't know just what you are suffering, but I know a little bit about troubles for the Lord. Let me tell you about something that happened when I was your age.

GRANDSON: Oh, Grandfather, that was so many years ago! Things were different then.

GRANDFATHER: Don't you think I was afraid when I was a

boy? Or don't you think I worried about what my friends would say? Things weren't so different. But sit down, and let me tell you. *(Lights begin to dim.)* In those days, many, many years ago, most of our people worshiped the spirits and the evil gods. The Medicine Man had much power in our village. Every week he would demand many sacrifices so that the spirits would be happy and not harm us. Back of our village there was a high hill. The Medicine Man said that this hill was sacred to the spirits. No one but the Medicine Man was allowed to climb this hill. No one was allowed to chop the wood or to touch anything on the sacred hill. The Medicine Man had the village in his power, and we feared him greatly.

Well, one day a missionary came to our village. I and my best friend, Olu, went to hear the missionary. Every day we visited the missionary. At first we did it secretly, and then we did it openly. The people in the village laughed at us. Some of them threw rocks at us, for they said we would bring harm to them. But we listened to the missionary carefully and were happy with the news we heard—the news that God loves us.

(Curtain closes.)

(SCENE TWO: *Village scene is shown. Sacred hill is at side opposite the village. Enter Shola and Olu.*)

SHOLA: Olu, those words that the missionary speaks, they fill my heart with joy.

OLU: Do not speak so loudly. Perhaps someone will hear!

SHOLA: I shall shout it! *The missionary tells about Jesus, and I love Jesus and will follow His path!* There, I have shouted it.

OLU: I love Jesus, too, friend Shola. But be careful. The Medicine Man has promised death to any who follow Jesus.

SHOLA: Then I shall die for Jesus. I will walk the Jesus path.

OLU: You will walk it alone. I will walk it, too, but not so others can know. I do not want to die. *(Exits.)*

(Medicine Man enters.)

MEDICINE MAN *(dancing and chanting)*: Ayah, ayah, ahahah. Ayah, on you is the curse of the sacred mountain. Ayah, on you is the curse of the sacred mountain. You shall die! Shola shall die, Shola shall die! Your flesh will wither and your eyes drop out. Your skin will wrinkle and your heart will stop. You will die! Die! Die! Shola will die!

SHOLA: Your curses can't hurt me. I am not afraid of you. I believe in the Lord Jesus Christ, and He died to save me. Medicine Man, Jesus loves you. He even loves *you!* And He wants you to quit sinning and to follow Him.

MEDICINE MAN: Ayah, ayah, ahahahah! On you is the curse. On you is the death. On you is the fear. On you is the trouble. You will die! Die! Die!

SHOLA: Tonight, Medicine Man, I am going to climb your sacred mountain. I am going to go up that mountain, and you and all the people in the village cannot stop me. I will go up that mountain, and then all the people in the village will know that Jesus is powerful and that He is the Lord God and that they should worship Him.

MEDICINE MAN: You will die! Die! Die! *(Exits dancing and chanting.)*

(Curtain closes.)

(SCENE THREE: *Curtain opens. Only the back curtain is shown. Grandfather and Grandson appear again.*)

GRANDSON: Oh, Grandfather, what happened? I know that there is a mountain back of our village that used to be worshiped and feared. I have heard you speak of it. But what happened? Weren't you afraid?

GRANDFATHER: Yes, Grandson, I was afraid. But in my heart I loved the Lord Jesus. I did not know what the Medicine Man would do to me. But I wanted everyone in the town to know that the Lord Jesus loved them and that He is the powerful One. Let me tell you what happened on that night so long ago.

(SCENE FOUR: *Lights dim. Curtain opens, with blue spotlight to represent night. Same scene as Scene Two.*)

SHOLA (*enters from side opposite sacred mountain*): Oh, my back hurts! It is so dark and so lonely. I—I am afraid.

OLU (*enters behind Shola and touches him on shoulder*): Shola!

SHOLA (*jumps, frightened*): Oh, Olu, you frightened me! Be careful. Do not put your weight on my shoulder.

OLU: What happened? What happened, my friend, Shola?

SHOLA: Ap! This afternoon I told my father that I would climb the sacred mountain tonight. And he beat me. Feel the bruises on my back.

OLU: My friend, Shola, you are hurt! Your back, your poor back! (*As he speaks, he is feeling the other puppet's back.*)

SHOLA: I told my father that I loved the Lord Jesus and that I did not fear his whip or the curses of the Medicine Man. That is why he whipped me so hard. But, friend Olu, what are *you* doing out here?

OLU: I, too, have spoken for the Lord Jesus. I told my father that I loved the Lord Jesus and that I would walk the Jesus path. Father listened carefully and said that he had been thinking about the words of the missionary. He has listened secretly as the missionary told of Jesus. My father said that he would like to follow the Lord Jesus, but that his heart feared. So I told him that tonight we would prove to him that Jesus was more powerful than the spirits of the sacred mountain.

SHOLA: Are you— Are you—

OLU: Yes, my friend, I am going with you. And if you die, then I will die. I will die for the Lord Jesus because He died for me! But, Shola, I am afraid.

SHOLA: And I, too, am afraid. Come, let us pray and ask Jesus to give us courage.

(Puppets bow their heads and are quiet for a few seconds.)

SHOLA: Now, let's climb that mountain! Just think, we will be the first from our village to climb it.

OLU: We may be the first from our village to die there, too! *(Spotlight is on, very dim. Black light comes on. The boys approach the hill slowly.)*

OLU: It is a frightful place!

(Shola begins to climb. This is done by moving the puppets slowly up the back of the cardboard hill. Occasionally one of the puppets slips, and the other helps him.)

SHOLA: It is very steep. My grandfather has told me that the Medicine Man has brought up many of his magic charms and hidden them on this hill.

OLU: If we step on one of them, perhaps we will die!

SHOLA: It is not the charm that I fear; it is the snake!

OLU: Oh, I wish you hadn't reminded me of that. It's so dark and scary!

SHOLA: But the Lord Jesus will help us. We want others to know that they should not follow the words of the Medicine Man. *(He groans.)*

OLU: What is the matter? Is it your back?

SHOLA: Yes, it is very sore, and some of these branches rub against it.

OLU: Maybe we'd better do this some other time. Let's go back.

SHOLA: No, I will do this tonight, so that everyone will know about the Lord Jesus.

(Drumming sounds begin. This can be tapping on a box backstage or could be a very soft recording of African drums. Occasionally soft cries are heard, to represent the people shouting to their spirit gods.)

OLU: What's that? What—what is happening?

SHOLA: Look, down there in the village! I can see a fire in the center of town. I think—yes, it is the Medicine Man. He has called the people together, and they are dancing and drumming for the spirits.

OLU: He wants the spirits to kill us. I'm afraid! What— what will— Oh, I— Oh!

SHOLA: Don't be afraid. We have asked the Lord Jesus to help us. Now, let's start to sing. We are at the top of the hill. Let's sing very loudly and let everyone know that we are here and that nothing has harmed us! Let's sing that song the missionary taught us, the one about Jesus loving us.

(NOTE: *If the children have been interested in a missionary who works in Africa, the missionary should be contacted*

*and asked to send the words to the song "Jesus Loves Me"
in the language of the people of that area. If this is not possible, the puppets could sing the following translation, which
is the Hausa language, one of the languages used in Nigeria
and in the Republic of Niger.)*

> Eee, yana *(yah-nah)* sona;
> Eee, yana sona;
> Eee, yana sona;
> Yesu, Mai-chetona *(my chay-toe-nah).*

(They repeat it several times and sing it also in English.)
(Curtain closes.)

(SCENE FIVE: *Curtain opens. Only back curtain is shown.
Grandfather and Grandson enter.)*

GRANDSON: It took a lot of courage to climb that mountain
when everyone thought that the spirits would kill you.
What happened, Grandfather?

GRANDFATHER: Olu and I sang all night long. We got cold
and sleepy, but we sang and shouted Bible verses all night
long. In the morning we went back down the hill—and
even carried some firewood with us from the sacred moun-
tainside!

GRANDSON: Was the Medicine Man angry?

GRANDFATHER: He was very angry. But when the people
saw us, they were happy. They realized that, if the spirits
couldn't kill two young boys, they weren't very powerful.
Many of the people stopped following the Medicine Man
and went to the missionary and learned about the Lord
Jesus.

GRANDSON: Grandfather, do you know what I'm going to

99

do? I'm going to Garba's house. I know that he likes my new top. I'm going to show it to him and help him make one just like it. I'm going to be friends with him, and I'm going to tell him that Christians aren't cowards. I'm going to tell him what you and your friend, Olu, did.

Even if he makes fun of me, I'm going to tell him about the Lord Jesus. I'm going to be brave for the Lord Jesus. *(Grandson exits. Curtain closes.)*

9

South American Missionary Play

ORO: young Indian boy

PEDRO: young school boy

MISSIONARY: man or woman, American or South
   American

FARMER

MINER

FISHERMAN

At least three puppeteers are needed. One puppeteer
manipulates and speaks for Pedro. Another can manipulate
Oro and speak for him, as well as managing Farmer, Miner,
and Fisherman, if the puppeteer is good at voice changes.
The third manipulates the missionary.

COSTUMES

Oro and Pedro are dressed in shorts and simple shirts of
different colors. Farmer wears poncho over his shoulders.
Fisherman wears simple shirt and may carry blanket over
one shoulder. The Farmer and the Fisherman can be played

Fig. 9a. Scene throughout play

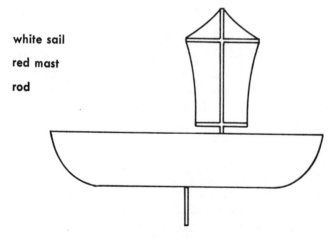

white sail

red mast

rod

Fig. 9b. Pedro's boat

by the same puppet with a quick change of clothes. Miner should wear blue pants and matching shirt and a hat.

PROPS

Scenery may be kept to a minimum; only a tree is really needed. The scene is the same throughout the play. See Figure 9a.

The boat may be either a child's sailboat or one made out of construction paper. It is mounted on a control rod. See Figure 9b. The mast must be red and cross-shaped; the sail is white.

ADAPTATION OF PLAY

This puppet play can be adapted to suit other countries by changing the boat to something appropriate to the country and giving the characters typical names. For Japan, the boat could be changed to a kite with the sins written on the kite tail. (See Fig. 9c.) The various characters could find the kite in different places. A balloon could be used for other countries, including Europe and America. Or it could be a sealed bottle cast into the river or ocean. The bottle would be washed up on the shore quickly because the child could not throw it far enough to have the waves carry it any distance.

(SCENE ONE: *Curtain opens to reveal Pedro beside the tree. He is working on his boat. Enter Oro.*)

ORO: Good morning, friend Pedro. I see you have returned from the big city. How do you like the escuela, the school?

PEDRO (*sadly*): Oh, si, I like the school very much.

103

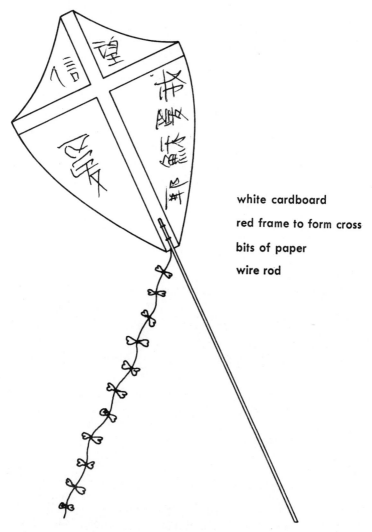

white cardboard

red frame to form cross

bits of paper

wire rod

Fig. 9c. Kite for Japanese version

ORO: But your voice sounds sad, Pedro, my friend. Are you sad?

PEDRO: Oh, si, I am very sad.

ORO: What makes your heart sad? Isn't your father the wealthiest cattle owner in the land? Do you not have a big hacienda and many horses?

PEDRO: But my heart is full of sin.

ORO: What makes you say that, amigo?

PEDRO: When I was in the big city at the school, one day I went for a walk to a part of town I did not know.

ORO: Si?

PEDRO: And I passed one small building. It was strange. I never had seen it before, and so I stood on the steps and looked in. Inside I saw a man standing in front of a crowd of people. He was talking to them.

ORO: And what did the hombre say? What did the man say, amigo Pedro?

PEDRO: He was telling the people that God was looking into their hearts and seeing sin.

ORO: Oh, si, everybody has sin.

PEDRO: But he was saying that God will punish everyone who has sin.

ORO: So you must go to the big church and make special prayers. Is that not what you do? Why did you not ask the man?

PEDRO: I wanted to ask him. But just then I looked at my watch and I saw that it was time for school. So I had to run.

ORO: But didn't you go to the big church?

PEDRO: Si, but even after I prayed, I still felt the sin in my heart. So I made a plan.

105

ORO: And what is that plan?

PEDRO: In all of South America *(change to country desired)* there is not such a plan as mine. I heard at the school that the ocean has so much water that no one can see the bottom.

ORO: And where is this ocean?

PEDRO: At school I was told this river goes into a bigger river, and that river goes into the ocean. So here is my plan. I have made a boat *(shows boat to Oro)*.

ORO: Your boat has wings on it, like the one we saw come up the river two moons ago. It is not like the boats our people use.

PEDRO: Si, my father says it travels with the wind. And I have written my sins on this paper. *(Shows him bottom of inside of boat. The paper may or may not be there, depending on the size of boat.)* All my sins are there. This boat will carry my sins to the ocean. There it will sink, and then my sins will be gone.

ORO: But why did you put your name on the boat?

PEDRO: I want the Creator God to know that this boat is carrying the sins of Pedro away.

ORO: Did you write down all your sins?

PEDRO: Si, all my sins.

ORO: Did you write about the time you hit me and made my nose bleed?

PEDRO: Si, I even wrote about that.

ORO: I hope you get rid of your sins. If you get rid of your sins, then you will not hit my nose again. Adios, amigo, I'm leaving you now.

(Oro exits.)

PEDRO: Si, it is a very good boat. I will put it here in the

106

water now, and it will carry my sins away. Good-bye, sins. Good-bye *(places boat in water)*.

(Boat sails away. This is done by lowering boat to level of stage and moving it away by means of the control rod beneath stage level. Make boat sail by moving boat toward side of stage and at same time raising and lowering it slightly. Curtain closes.)

(SCENE TWO: *Curtain opens a few seconds later to same scene. Pedro enters, head down, walking slowly.*)

PEDRO *(sadly)*: I hope my boat has reached the sea. I should be happy because my sins are gone. They are all gone. But I don't feel happy. My sins are gone. It has been one whole day since I let my boat loose on the river. But still my heart feels sad.

(Farmer enters with boat under arm.)

PEDRO: Who—who are you? What—what are you doing?

FARMER: Last night I was working on my garden, and I got tired. So I went to the river to wash and rest. Ah, a very strange thing happened. This lovely little boat came into my hands. Eh, I cannot read, but I saw that it has much writing on it, so I took it to the storekeeper. He said it has the name *Pedro* on it. He said he knows a Pedro who lives in this village. Do you know Pedro?

PEDRO *(sadly)*: I am Pedro. I am Pedro. That is my boat.

FARMER: It is a very good boat, and I know you are sad that your boat got lost. I am glad I can bring it to you. Now I must go. Here is your boat *(hands boat to Pedro)*.

PEDRO *(sadly)*: Thank you.

(Farmer exits.)

PEDRO: That is not all you brought to me. Oh, yes, you

brought me much trouble. You returned my sins to me. Now I must let it go again. Please, boat, please take my sins to the deepest part of the ocean *(releases boat)*.
(Boat sails away. Curtain closes.)

(SCENE THREE: *Curtain opens to reveal Pedro under the tree. He is sad.*)

PEDRO: Three hours have passed. My boat must have reached the sea by now. Surely by now it is in the bottom of the ocean. My sins are all gone. They are in the ocean. Oh, Señor, what have you got there?

(Miner enters.)

MINER: I am looking for one niño named Pedro. Surely this is Pedro's boat. It is the boat of a child.

PEDRO: I am Pedro.

MINER: I was panning the stream, hoping to find a bit of yellow gold, and this came into my gold pan. I was coming back to the village for supplies, and so I brought it to you. Pedro, you do not look very happy. I am not asking for a reward.

PEDRO: Si, Señor, I know. I thank you very much for returning my boat. You are too kind. Gracias.

(Miner gives Pedro the boat and exits.)

PEDRO: He has returned all my sins. I must try again. Please, boat, do not go into any miner's gold pan. Go to the depths of the ocean *(sails boat)*.

(Curtain closes.)

(SCENE FOUR: *Curtain opens. Pedro is at same place.*)

PEDRO: Ah, the sun is about to set, and my boat has not returned. I shall sleep in peace tonight knowing—

108

(Fisherman enters with boat.)

FISHERMAN: Pedro, I have found your boat.

(Pedro runs and tries to hide behind small tree.)

FISHERMAN: Pedro, don't you hear me? This is your boat; I caught it in my net. *(Looks around tree, and Pedro darts in back of him.)* Pedro, what is the matter with you? *(Catches him and hands him boat.)*

PEDRO: Oh si, yes, my boat. Ah—ah—thank you, gracias.

FISHERMAN: One would think you weren't happy to see your lovely boat. Eh, who can know a child? *(Exits.)*

PEDRO: Sins! How can I get rid of them? My father prays to all the idols in our house. My mother longs to go on a pilgrimage. Eh, my heart is sad. The medicine man of the Indians tells me that I must kill chickens. Everyone tells me something different. Well, boat, this is the only way I know; my sins are written here.

But one thing I know, I will not take the boat back *(sails boat)*.

(Curtain closes.)

(SCENE FIVE: *Pedro is alone.*)

PEDRO: Last night I dreamed that everyone in the world brought my boat back to me. But I know it is gone now. I have not seen it since last night. I know my sins are—
(Missionary enters. Pedro bows to the ground and hides face.)

MISSIONARY: I have been told that you are Pedro *(waits for an answer; no response)*. I sought you in the village, and I was told you were here by the river's edge *(no response)*. I have brought your beautiful boat *(no response)*. Don't you want your boat? It *is* your boat?

PEDRO (*in dead, flat voice*): Si, Señor (Senorita), it is my boat. Gracias, thank you.

MISSIONARY: You sound very sad. I am a missionary. I have brought your boat to you.

PEDRO: Thank you. Thank you, Missionary.

MISSIONARY: You sound sad.

PEDRO: Thank you, I am sad.

MISSIONARY: You didn't want your boat?

PEDRO: Thank you, I didn't want my boat.

MISSIONARY: It is a fine boat.

PEDRO: Thank you, it is a fine boat.

MISSIONARY: But you never wanted to see it again?

PEDRO: Yes, I never wanted to see it again.

MISSIONARY: Listen, amigo, I have not only brought your beautiful boat to you, but I have brought you the true news of how you can get rid of your sins.

PEDRO (*shows interest by standing upright and speaking more cheerfully*): You have brought me that news? Thank you, Missionary, this is good. How can I get rid of my sins?

MISSIONARY: I want to tell you about the Lord Jesus Christ who came into the world to die for your sins, to take them all away. Jesus is God's Son, and He paid for your sins. He loves you and wants you to love and obey Him.

PEDRO: This is indeed good news. Please, perhaps you would come to my house and tell my father and mother about this good news? Come.

(They exit. Curtain closes.)

(SCENE SIX: *Curtain opens to empty stage. Enter Pedro and Oro. Pedro is carrying boat.*)

110

ORO: I see that you have your boat with you yet. Have you not gotten rid of your sins? I thought you would sail your boat to the ocean.

PEDRO: My sins are taken away! They are buried deeper than the deepest ocean. They are all gone!

ORO: But—I see your boat! How did this happen? Are you going to sail your boat?

PEDRO: I am going to sail my boat, but only for fun. Just for fun. But as I sail the boat, it reminds me of something. See the mast and sail? The red mast reminds me of the cross on which Jesus died to pay for my sins. And the white sail reminds me that, since I believe in Jesus, my sins are washed away.

ORO: But what of your sins that were written on the paper in the boat?

PEDRO: Ah, those! I burned that silly paper. I should have known better—but I didn't. Now I know that only Jesus can take sins away. Come, Oro, I want you to hear all that the missionary told us. My mother and father have believed in Jesus, too. Now I want to tell you.

(Both exit. Curtain closes.)

DATE DUE